THE
MITCHEL LONDON
GRACIE MANSION
COOKBOOK

MITCHEL LONDON *and* JOAN SCHWARTZ
Foreword by Edward I. Koch, Mayor of New York City

CONTEMPORARY
BOOKS

CHICAGO · NEW YORK

Library of Congress Cataloging-in-Publication Data

London, Mitchel.
    The Mitchel London Gracie Mansion cookbook / Mitchel London and
  Joan Schwartz : foreword by Edward Koch.
       p.   cm.
  Includes index.
  ISBN 0-8092-4472-1 : $19.95
  1. Cookery, French.   I. Schwartz, Joan, 1938–   II. Title.
TX719.L66   1989
641.5944—dc20   89-7185
                                                  CIP

Published by Contemporary Books, Inc.
180 North Michigan Avenue, Chicago, Illinois 60601
Manufactured in the United States of America
Library of Congress Catalog Card Number: 89-7185
International Standard Book Number: 0-8092-4472-1

Published simultaneously in Canada by Beaverbooks, Ltd.
195 Allstate Parkway, Valleywood Business Park
Markham, Ontario L3R 4T8 Canada

Dedicated to
my mother, Elaine London, the best cook I know,
and to the memory of my father, Philip London;

to the extraordinary Schwartzes,
Allen, David, Rachel, and Deborah;

and to the finest Mayor New York City has ever had,
Edward I. Koch

Contents

Foreword   *vii*

Nutritionist's Preface   *xi*

Acknowledgments   *xv*

Introduction   *xvii*

PART 1: BASICS

Methods   *3*

Vegetables and Herbs in Food Preparation   *17*

Stocks   *31*

PART 2: RECIPES

Appetizers   *41*

Soups   *55*

Pasta   *67*

Fish   *83*

Shellfish   *105*

Chicken   *119*

Veal   *131*

Lamb and Beef   *145*

Vegetables   *161*

Salads   *177*

Salad Dressings   *187*

Desserts   *195*

Thanksgiving   *205*

A Week of Well-Planned, Moderate Dinner Menus   *213*

Index   *217*

Foreword

Edward I. Koch
Mayor of the City of New York

Mitchel London is a chef extraordinaire.

If New York City is a melting pot, he has stirred and seasoned it to present only the best to our citizens and distinguished visitors. For seven years, Mitchel orchestrated an incredible array of tastes and met untold logistical challenges in responding to the myriad requests for official entertaining. Whether it was a late-night crisis or an impromptu cocktail reception, Mitchel's special energy and gastronomic expertise made discussion of some very tough municipal issues palatable—quite literally!

I doubt that anyone else could have worked as hard, been as attentive to my culinary needs, or been as available to prepare meals at the odd hours I have dinner during the week—not to mention providing full-course meals at the drop of a hat for me and my spur-of-the-moment guests or catering a state dinner for 125 guests or more.

Mitchel London was hired as the chef at Gracie Mansion in 1981, after we had gone through five chefs. We asked all candidates for the job to prepare a meal as part of their application process. The highlight of the dinner that Mitchel prepared was Osso Buco (see Index), which contained more garlic than any Osso Buco I had ever tasted. I loved it! He had met my high culinary standards.

Garlic is an extremely healthful food. I sometimes say that my total recovery from a stroke in August 1987 may have resulted from the enormous amounts of garlic that I consumed during the course of the year. (I must add that to avoid social ostracism, I eat cooked garlic, which is milder than raw. It must work; I cannot document a single case of anyone withdrawing in horror upon close contact.) I jocularly tell people that my passion for garlic goes back to the pre-vaccine days when one way to prevent polio was to wear garlic around your neck or, at the very least, mothballs. So much for primitive medicine!

This book is intended to provide delicious but light recipes and menus to the enormous number of people who want to be thin, of whom I am one. I want to make it clear that I'm not obese! It's just that I have this image of myself that goes back to when I was twenty-two years old and weighed 180 pounds instead of 215, as I currently do.

Although Mitchel was always willing to accommodate my request that he cook lean and mean, I believe he concluded that in the end it was best to keep me happy. And happiness for me, while it includes a whole host of other activities, also includes eating a fine dinner—sometimes, regrettably, one filled with calories.

When I asked, "Can't we have pasta?" or "Can't we have pasta with bacon, sun-dried tomatoes, and a cream sauce?" his response was "Are you sure that's what you want, Mayor?" When I said, "Yes," he created the dish in all its glory. I wouldn't have had it otherwise.

Mitchel is unique, and I wish him the best. The question in my mind is, now that he has left, will I gain weight as a result of eating between meals, which Mitchel never allowed me to do?

Nutritionist's Preface

Maureen Callahan, M.S., R.D.

That the link between diet and health is strong is no longer a debatable matter. In the summer of 1988, the Surgeon General issued a landmark report on nutrition that confirmed the connection between the typical American diet—replete with rich, premium ice creams, fatty meat, and buttery pastries—and diseases such as cancer, hypertension, heart disease, and stroke. Simply put, his message concluded: Americans eat too much, particularly too much fat and saturated fat.

Of course, that message is not new. Many Americans have been trying to do something about trimming the fat and calories from meals for years. Mitchel London, chef at Gracie Mansion from 1981 to 1988, counts himself as one of that group. After Mayor Ed Koch's stroke, Mitchel made it a point to lower the fat, cholesterol, and calorie content of Mansion recipes whenever possible. Mitchel followed no rigid practice of counting numbers of calories or grams of fat but rather took a more commonsense approach to using healthful ingredients and smaller amounts of food high in fat and saturated fat. For example, a classic pureed mussel soup was lightened by removing cream and butter from the recipe, thus lowering fat and calorie content. The lightened soup is as delicious as the classic version.

While *Mitchel London's Gracie Mansion Cookbook* is not strictly health-oriented, many of these recipes are indeed healthful. Nowhere in the book will you find an analysis of numbers of calories or grams of fat in a recipe. Instead, we have used a coding system to let you know which recipes are lower in fat and calories. "Light" recipes are those with little or no fat added. They are preceded by this symbol: ♣ . Dishes labeled "moderate" are made with a little more fat than can be considered light but are a good transition toward lower fat. They are labeled: ♣♣ . Those dishes labeled "rich" are preceded by this symbol:♣♣♣. They would be for occasional indulgences, since they contain larger amounts of fat.

In the dessert section, "light" and "moderate" reflect sugar content. Three fruit desserts are labeled "moderate" and one is labeled "rich," although they are entirely fat free.

As a nutritionist, I give high ratings to such recipes as the Extra-Light Dressing, Poached Salmon with Dill and Yogurt Sauce, and Mussels in White Wine. Though these dishes contain little or no fat, they taste delicious. But there is no need to eat only the light recipes from this book. If you are eating a high-fat entree, such as Grilled Butterflied Leg of Lamb, accompany it with no- or low-fat side dishes, such as the Mélange of Steamed Vegetables and tangy Grapefruit Sorbet.

One final word: some recipes do call for butter (trying to get a chef trained in the classic cuisine to forgo butter is virtually impossible), but amounts are usually small. But for people who are scrupulous about other sources of saturated fat—that is, you buy lean meat, pull the skin off chicken, seldom eat rich bakery goods—a little bit of butter should not be harmful. After all, conventional nutritional wisdom aims for balance.

Congratulations to Mitchel for meeting the challenge of combining health with pleasurable eating. He turns the tables on indulgence and works magic with spices, seasonings, and everyday foods, converting them into sumptuous salads, main courses, and desserts that people would never suspect are good for them.

Acknowledgments

We would like to thank David Reese, curator of the Gracie Mansion Conservancy, for generously providing information on the history and restoration of Gracie Mansion.

Introduction

The book you are about to read is a collection of my special recipes, those prepared during the time I served as chef to New York's Mayor Ed Koch at Gracie Mansion. I'm sure you have read longer books, with more extensive recipe lists, and so have I. But my intention in writing this cookbook was not to present the entire world of cuisine once over lightly. Readers don't need yet another recipe for a quiche or another diagram for boning a chicken breast. I haven't padded this book with recipes you can find just about anywhere. I have given you recipes for the dishes I cooked again and again at Gracie Mansion. I have also introduced you to my style of cooking: I use the best seasonal ingredients I can find, and I prepare them with a minimum of fuss but with élan. I do not arrange food into picture-book constructions. I serve food so that it speaks for itself, showing off its natural beauty and appeal.

This is a commonsense book for people who love good food and want to prepare it quickly. I encourage you to use your own good judgment in food choice and preparation. No matter how much you enjoy being in the kitchen (and I very much enjoy it), I don't want to keep you there when your guests and family are waiting for your company. I hope I can get you into and out of the kitchen efficiently.

This is also a book for people who want to lighten their diets, as so many of us now do. It is easy—or reasonably easy—to put together fantastic dishes using butter, cream, and egg yolks. I have found it is just as easy to do so without relying on them. I hope I have given you a cookbook you will use often and make a part of your life.

The recipes and techniques that follow served me well through seven years at Gracie Mansion. They are tried and true. You will find nothing here that does not work; nothing that has not pleased a variety of guests; nothing extraneous. The recipes have all been tested on a discerning and demanding clientele.

Many of the dishes I include take half an hour from kitchen to dining table. Some of my favorites, like pastas, are even quicker. During the years I worked for him, Mayor Ed Koch had a busy and often unpredictable schedule. Dinner at 7:00 could turn out to be dinner at 8:00 or even dinner at 11:00. I could not prepare the main course until the Mayor walked through the door, but usually I was able to serve him dinner within 15 minutes of his arrival. I have adapted my methods for the home cook and offer you the benefit of my years of kitchen experience. Of course, most home kitchens differ somewhat from professional kitchens (I will describe the Gracie Mansion kitchen later), and you may find that you have to add a few minutes to my preparation time. But you will still find that my focus is on efficiency. I have pared down my recipes and stressed common sense in food preparation.

In the summer of 1987, the Mayor suffered a slight stroke (in his words, "slight to my doctors"). He felt it would be a good idea to lose some weight and to rid his diet of cholesterol-producing fats. He did not want to count calories strictly, but he knew a lighter diet was in the best interest of his overall good health. He asked me to lighten his menu, without sacrificing the elegance and flavor he expected for himself and his guests.

I was classically trained as a chef, and I favor rich, traditional dishes. Like the Mayor, I love to eat. I was reluctant to tie my daily menu planning to nutrition charts, calorie counts, and food exchanges. I asked myself, "How can I have my cake and eat it too?" I felt the answer lay in common sense and moderation, and I decided to try the idea of food balance. It seemed sensible to me that even a dieter need not restrict himself to Spartan meals. A meal is made up of several elements. If most of these are lean and light, then there is room for a little luxury in the meal as a whole. For instance, the great chef Michel Guérard has a marvelous recipe for Chicken Stuffed Under the Skin with Farmer Cheese. This is a rich dish, and you wouldn't have it every night. But if you had it for dinner one evening, and if the rest of the dinner were very carefully planned, you could eat this chicken with a clear conscience. I served it as a part of the following menu:

Mayor Koch's Favorite Pureed Mussel Soup*
Chicken Stuffed Under the Skin with Farmer Cheese*
Steamed Haricots Verts*
Orange Sorbet*

You don't feel that you are being overly careful with a meal like this. All the other elements set off and highlight the beautiful main course. Balance is a key concept aesthetically as well as medically.

_____

*See Index for recipes.

During a recent visit to France, I had the pleasure of dining in four-star restaurants (Tailevant, Alain Chapel, and Paul Bocuse) and a two-star restaurant (Guy Savoy). Because I chose to eat sensibly, I never felt that I had overeaten. Let me assure you that I really denied myself nothing. The meals I put together were fabulous, but not ridiculously rich.

A recent survey agrees with my approach. A spokesperson for the National Heart, Lung, and Blood Institute summed up its results by saying: "It's your overall diet that's important, and that isn't emphasized as often as it should be." Of course, I also modify individual dishes and keep lightness in mind as a guiding principle.

The American public has benefited from what amounts to an information explosion concerning stroke and heart attack prevention, cholesterol control, and dietary guidelines. These topics have become so much a part of our thinking about food that recipes offered even in fairly recent cookbooks have become unacceptable to many cooks. In this book I use the finest ingredients, fresh herbs, and natural sauces and reductions. I limit but do not entirely eliminate salt, egg yolks, and butter—with these ingredients, a little goes a long way, and used sparingly, they can make the difference between tasty and tasteless food. And tasty food, after all, is what you want from this cookbook. Some dishes are rich, some dishes are light, and it is up to you as the cook to choose among them and put together healthful menus. This book is about eating well and appreciating fine food, but it is also about common sense, judgment, and moderation. These concepts worked well for me in Gracie Mansion.

In planning meals I included recipes that ranged from especially light (Mayor Koch's Favorite Pureed Mussel Soup, Steamed Shrimp with Ginger, and Fettuccine with Tomato Sauce and Steamed Vegetables), to moderately light (Roasted Salmon, Veal Medallions with Morels, and Asparagus with Grilled Shrimp), to rich (Mussel Soup with Saffron, Chicken Stuffed Under the Skin with Farmer Cheese). I have indicated the relative lightness of all the recipes to help you in balancing your own menus.

When it comes to desserts, however, I get tough. The dessert section of this book is basic and to the point. After a satisfying and well-planned meal, the best dessert is fresh fruit in season. I give recipes for a few desserts using fruit, such as sorbets. However, I really believe that the freshest local strawberries in June or peaches in August are among the finest desserts you can offer your guests.

I discussed my concept of healthful eating and my recipes with nutritionist Maureen Callahan, who acted as consultant on the dishes in this book.

As I said earlier, I am a classically trained chef. I was born in Philadelphia and was graduated from the American International School in Israel. While in school I ran the kiosk (and was also the assistant gym teacher).

Part of my early food experience was managing the House of Ice Cream in north Tel Aviv and working at the Osteria d'Antonio in that famous center of Italian cooking, Herzliya. I decided early that I wanted to cook professionally. (Even now, I love cooking and am often restless out of the kitchen. Writing this book with Joan Schwartz, I often found myself fidgeting while talking and writing about food. I wanted to get back into the kitchen and actually cook—not waste my time with words.)

I returned home and enrolled in the Culinary Department of the Rhode Island School of Design (RISD), where I received excellent training. After graduation in 1977, I stayed on and taught at RISD for two years. On the side, I organized the food service for the Grace Church retirement apartments and supplied the Brown University Faculty Club with brioches. I worked as a summer camp chef, and I spent two glorious months touring and "tasting" France.

I have tried to repeat that experience every summer. I enjoy renting a house in the south of France and experimenting with the wonderful French foods and wines. Provence has influenced my style of cooking, which makes abundant use of fresh herbs and wonderful seasonal fruits and vegetables.

On a typical summer day in the Côte d'Azur, I find myself shopping for food three times: before breakfast, lunch, and dinner. Here, this would be excessive, but it is common practice in that part of France. The market is a short trip by ferry, giving me fifteen minutes of one of the most beautiful views in the world. I buy the freshest bread three times a day and the freshest produce when it comes into the market.

It takes a few days after my arrival to get the kitchen set up, but after that meals are bliss. For breakfast, I serve fresh juice, baguettes, a mild cheese, and my own preserves made from white peaches. Lunch is often pasta with fresh herbs and a dessert of fresh fruit. Dinner is some kind of grilled fish or perhaps grilled lamb (the only red meat I care for in France—fish is more reliable).

One of my favorite places to buy food in the south of France is the glorious fish market in St. Tropez—a long, shaded corridor full of cool marble tables displaying the freshest of fish. No matter how hot the day, it is cool here. The fish have all been caught that morning; the market closes for the day at 10:00 A.M.

There are so many varieties of fish, many of which are not available in the United States, that I can never choose only one. I generally buy two or three types at a time because they are so irresistible. It is hard to make up your mind when you see fresh Dover sole, loup, sardines, and langoustines, to name just a few.

I take the fish home and grill them outdoors over a wood fire. They are so fresh and perfect, you can usually just throw them on the grill. You haven't lived until you have tasted perfectly fresh little sardines, grilled au naturel. One of my favorite menus is the following:

Grilled Sardines*
Grilled Lamb Chops
Green Salad
Wild Strawberries

We always serve fish grilled, and we eat many beautiful salads. Among the other glories of summer are the white peaches, the strawberries, the tomatoes, and the melons. And of course, the Côte de Provence rose wine.

This is the kind of food and the kind of cooking I enjoy most, and whenever possible I tried to transplant it to New York and Gracie Mansion.

To get back to my story: I was in California visiting a friend, when my brother called to tell me that there was a job available as Mayor Koch's chef. I applied for the job, and the Mayor and his staff were interested in my application. I flew back from California to be interviewed and to cook a meal. Here is the menu that opened a new chapter in my life:

Mussels in White Wine*
Angel Hair Pasta with Cream, Lemon, and Vodka Sauce
Osso Buco*
Roasted Peppers*
Chocolate Mousse-Meringue Cake

Of course, this was before the enlightenment, but the menu translates remarkably well. Mussels in white wine are an excellent way to start a light meal. Although Osso Buco is rich and flavorful, it contains no butter or cream. It is made with light olive oil and natural veal stock. The pasta can stay, but the cream must go. Forget you ever heard of chocolate mousse-meringue cake. I would serve this menu today as follows:

Mussels in White Wine*
Pasta with Shiitake Mushrooms*
Osso Buco*
Roasted Peppers*
Strawberries with Raspberry Puree*

This menu is a fine example of how to lighten a classic meal without sacrificing elegance or flavor. I still find this a wonderful dinner, and it is

---

*See Index for recipes.

easy to prepare. It exemplifies the message of this book: how to eat sensibly but well.

I don't think most people would have prepared this menu as part of an employment application, because Osso Buco is hardly a common dish. But it was delicious and impressive, and I got the job.

The job was described to me as follows: The office of mayor required considerable entertaining of dignitaries in small, informal dinners and larger, more formal parties and receptions. The Mayor gave many small dinner parties, and he gave large dinner parties for about one hundred people about once a month. Receptions (drinks and hors d'oeuvres) for about 250 people were held about once every two weeks. There were breakfast meetings with aides about once a week. (Later, there were a few more receptions, and I also prepared lunches at City Hall for eight to twelve people. But the job did not change in essence.)

All this sounded exciting and challenging, and I was eager to be chosen. The possibility of working for the Mayor of the world's most fascinating city intrigued me. New York may not be the true center of the universe, but it certainly attracts a lot of attention. I had never been especially interested in politics or government, and I would not have pursued a job in the kitchen of any other mayor. But this was New York and the legendary Mayor Ed Koch. I knew working at Gracie Mansion would have to be exciting.

When I met Mayor Koch, I was delighted to find him easygoing and unpretentious. Plus, I had always heard that he loved to eat. I knew I would fit well in the Gracie Mansion kitchen. Over the years, my expectations were happily fulfilled.

People have since asked me if I would ever work for another mayor. I always give the same answer: I wouldn't cook for another mayor; I wouldn't make coffee for another mayor; I wouldn't boil water for another mayor. I am strongly loyal to Mayor Koch.

Although I was originally hired as the cook, a number of staff and administration changes were made in the course of time, and eventually I became executive administrator, as well as chef. As executive administrator, I worked with a staff that varied from about eight to eighteen people. I was responsible for purchasing and preparation of food; for party planning; and for seeing that the silver, table, bar, and so on were taken care of. Something a little harder to pin down, which goes with all of this, was my responsibility for the general plan of the evening. Working around the Mayor's often changeable schedule, I saw that the meal was on time, that each course took up its proper portion of time—not too long and not too short—and that the event flowed easily. Sometimes the Mayor was more impatient than I. I learned that whenever he asked me how long something would take, my standard, safe answer was "5 minutes." Then I tried my best to conform to my answer. I recall one summer dinner when I told the Mayor the guests could sit down in the dining room in 10 minutes, and the Mayor advised me that it would be better to sit *now*. I think we split the difference.

One of the first bits of advice I received when I began working was to have lots of tuna-fish salad handy, because the Mayor loved it. Consequently, I served the Mayor lots of tuna-fish salad, and he seemed to love it. Then I learned he was just being polite. A previous chef had served it to him, advised the subsequent chef that he liked it, and so on, until the myth was born. Fortunately, the myth was laid to rest during my tenure, and I served the Mayor lots of pasta. I think he loved it.

The job of the Mayor of New York is a very demanding one, and it requires an efficiently functioning household for receptions, breakfasts, luncheons, and dinners of state. Of course, even with the best of planning and execution, even the perfect household sometimes can disappoint its guests. When I had not been at Gracie Mansion for very long, I made a luncheon for President Sandro Pertini of Italy, to which about one hundred dignitaries were invited. We spent days planning the perfect menu and finally came up with:

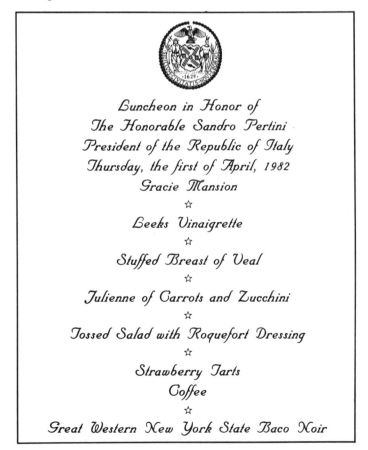

Luncheon in Honor of
The Honorable Sandro Pertini
President of the Republic of Italy
Thursday, the first of April, 1982
Gracie Mansion
☆
Leeks Vinaigrette
☆
Stuffed Breast of Veal
☆
Julienne of Carrots and Zucchini
☆
Tossed Salad with Roquefort Dressing
☆
Strawberry Tarts
Coffee
☆
Great Western New York State Baco Noir

I am still impressed by this menu. Most of the guests were pleased, but apparently the guest of honor was less so. President Pertini politely asked for cheese and fruit. This is one way to lighten your meals, if you are so inclined.

My meal planning reflected the Mayor's taste, as well as my own experience and preferences. The usual dinner party for ten to fifteen people was much less formal than the luncheon just mentioned. It generally included four hors d'oeuvres served as accompaniments to drinks. One of the simplest and best of these is my Broiled Tomato Sandwich: For each sandwich, cover a slice of good Italian bread with a slice of ripe tomato. Top with a slice of goat cheese and drizzle with olive oil. Run under the broiler until brown. Top with a basil leaf.

The Mayor had always enjoyed rather caloric hors d'oeuvres, but after he decided to lighten his diet, I felt that they would be easy to cut back on. In my opinion, hors d'oeuvres, while they should be delicious, should never be overdone or too time-consuming, even though they are part of the larger picture, the well-planned meal. I sometimes think of hors d'oeuvres as a pleasant way to fill the time waiting for late-arriving guests.

Crudités began to appear regularly as hors d'oeuvres, with a lot of daikon, the Mayor's favorite. I used fresh carrots, peppers, cauliflower, broccoli—whatever looked really beautiful in the market. For a dip, I combined yogurt and chopped fresh dill or other herbs. Two other hors d'oeuvres enjoyed by guests were Grilled Salmon Chunks with ginger and Bruschetta alla Romana (see Index).

It would be hard to make an uninteresting dinner or luncheon party at the Mayor's home. As guests arrive, they are immediately enchanted by the setting and the house. Gracie Mansion is an inspiring place in which to entertain and be entertained. Guests feel they are a part of New York's history as they sit among the art and artifacts of this beautifully restored house.

Located in New York City's Carl Schurz Park, overlooking the East River, Gracie Mansion looks like the stately nineteenth-century country house it originally was. The house was built in 1799 by Archibald Gracie, a New York merchant, and was subsequently owned by the Foulke and Wheaton families. The city took possession of the house and property in 1896 but made little use of it until 1923. From 1923 to 1932, it housed the Museum of the City of New York. It has been the official residence of the Mayor of the City of New York since 1942, when Fiorello La Guardia moved in.

In 1984 the Gracie Mansion Conservancy completed renovation of the house, making it, in the Mayor's words, "a house in which all New Yorkers can take pride." This landmark home, authentically restored, is now a practical place to live and work. Among Mayor Koch's guests at the

Mansion have been Presidents Carter and Reagan, Premier Zhao Ziyang of the People's Republic of China, French Prime Minister Jacques Chirac, President Sandro Pertini of Italy, and Prime Minister Menachem Begin of Israel. Such artists as Marilyn Horne, Sherrill Milnes, Benny Goodman, and Michael Feinstein have performed on the "Live from Gracie Mansion" programs on WNYC-FM.

Large formal parties and receptions are held in the Susan E. Wagner Wing, an addition to the original house completed in 1966. The wing consists of an entrance hall, a ballroom seating up to 150 people, a sitting room, and a library, all decorated in Federal style and furnished with beautiful antiques and paintings from the eighteenth and nineteenth centuries, many lent by New York City's museums.

Smaller parties take place in the original house, where the Mayor lives. The spacious center hall has been restored, with a dramatic floor painted to resemble marble and a majestic stairway leading to the upstairs bedrooms. It contains a Sheraton settee from 1815–20 on loan from the City Art Commission, and a New York tall clock, among other authentic pieces of furniture and art lent or donated by city institutions and private citizens.

At our winter dinner parties, we served hors d'oeuvres to guests who were enjoying the warmth of the cheerful fireplaces in the library or parlor. (The house, incidentally, has fourteen fireplaces.) Both rooms offer a feast for the antique lover and the history buff.

The parlor is the more formal of the two rooms, featuring a marble mantelpiece bought in France in the 1820s by Joseph Foulke, the second owner of the house. The elegant blue and gold wallpaper in this room is a copy of a French wallpaper of the same period. Much of the parlor furniture is in the style of the late Federal period (1810–25) and several pieces, such as the Duncan Phyfe eagle-back side chairs and the secretary, are originals on loan from the Museum of the City of New York. The comfortable "Grecian" sofa is a copy of Duncan Phyfe's style, and other upholstered pieces are in the style of the late nineteenth century.

Some other outstanding pieces of furniture are the chest of drawers by Michael Allison, dating from about 1810, a Steinway "parlor grand" piano made in 1872, an 1840s gas chandelier, and an 1830s marble-topped center table.

These pieces are beautiful to look at and functional as well, making the room a most comfortable place for entertaining. Guests can also admire the paintings by New York artists on New York subject matter that were lent to the Gracie Mansion Conservancy by New York City's leading cultural institutions.

The library accommodates fairly small groups for hors d'oeuvres and conversation before dinner. The focal points of that room are the beautifully restored mantel of white carved wood and marble, which dates back to about 1799, and the Regency crystal chandelier dating back to about 1820. There are lovely and comfortable Sheraton arm and side chairs, in deep red and cream, as well as a cream-colored sofa, a pedestal table made by Meeks & Co., and beautiful mahogany bookcases. The library walls, like those of the parlor, are hung with paintings lent to the Gracie Mansion Conservancy.

After hors d'oeuvres, the Mayor's guests move into the dining room, a spacious, bright room whose walls are covered by magnificent 1830s wallpaper restored for Gracie Mansion. The paper depicts pastoral scenes in rich blues and greens. A sideboard from about 1815–20, probably made by the shop of Duncan Phyfe, stands against one wall. The dining table and chairs are reproductions of Federal-style furniture.

This is one menu I would have served in that lovely room on a particularly blustery winter night:

Pureed Vegetable Soup*
Roast Leg of Lamb*
Mélange of Steamed Vegetables*
Marinated Fruit*

Or I might have offered this menu later in the year:

Asparagus with Parmesan*
Salmon en Papillote*
Endive and Watercress Salad*
Poached Pears with Two Fruit Purees*

I found that guests at the Mansion enjoyed this meal:

Roasted Red and Yellow Peppers* with Balsamic Vinaigrette*
Leg of Lamb with Vegetables in One Pot*
Fennel with Bibb Lettuce* with Mustard Vinaigrette
Seasonal Fruit

Conversation at these dinners seemed to be lively and stimulating. I like to think it was helped along by the good food (not that Mayor Ed Koch needed any help).

In spring and summer, I often served breakfast and dinner on the porch. Guests overlooked the informal gardens, beautifully planned and maintained by Maureen Hackett, which are a rainbow of magnificent color. In

---

*See Index for recipes.

the spring, late daffodils, tulips, azaleas, dogwood, redbud, and grape hyacinth come into bloom, just to give you an idea of the variety. In the summer, the garden positively explodes with about forty different perennials and as many flowering annuals, plus assorted shrubs. Blue ageratum, Dahlborg daisies, signet marigolds, roses, petunias, shasta daisies, veronica, peonies, asters, and impatiens all provide a delicious menu for the eyes.

Hors d'oeuvres were served to guests who sat on outdoor furniture, accompanied by the sounds of the river and the park. For dinner, the guests moved to a dining table set up alfresco on another section of the large porch. They overlooked the grill in the backyard and watched the preparation of their food. Guests are somehow cheered and invigorated at the sight of a blazing grill standing ready. A popular summer menu was:

Grilled Marinated Tomatoes with Basil*
Grilled Marinated Tuna*
Steamed Snow Peas and Carrots*
Strawberries with Crème Fraîche (optional)

Most food, of course, was not cooked outdoors but was prepared in the Gracie Mansion kitchen. This kitchen is not large by professional standards; it is a somewhat compact, very efficient and workable room. The walls are lined with two industrial ranges, which have ten burners and a flat-top grill, as well as four ovens in all. There are generous work surfaces and a sink and work surface on a center island. Copper and iron pots and pans of various sizes are hung from the ceiling over the island.

The kitchen boasts an unusual wood-burning grill along one wall. This indoor grill was really essential to my light cooking—I was able to prepare any number of delicious dishes without extra fats, any time of the year.

There is also a small microwave oven, which I rarely used, except for defrosting. Two small auxiliary kitchens, attached to the main one, are used for cleanup and dishwashing.

The kitchen is located between the main house and the Susan E. Wagner ballroom and works well for both the smaller parties in the main house and the larger events in the ballroom.

Cooking for large dinners—that is, for parties of about one hundred guests—at Gracie Mansion was quite different from preparing small meals for ten to fifteen people. First of all, the Susan E. Wagner Wing is used for large groups because of its magnificent ballroom. Thus, the feeling immediately is formal rather than intimate. A large dinner involves a lot of careful planning, both culinary and budgetary. Naturally, the second

---

*See Index for recipes.

must influence the first, so the chef cannot be as creative as he might want to be. I always tried to make these large dinners as personal as I could and to avoid the stereotypical banquet food.

A menu for the king and queen of Sweden required some serious planning, and the result was simply magnificent. This was served in April 1988:

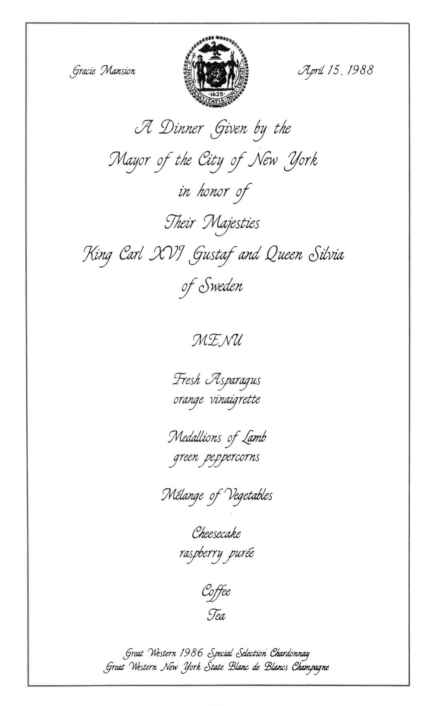

Gracie Mansion   April 15, 1988

A Dinner Given by the
Mayor of the City of New York
in honor of
Their Majesties
King Carl XVI Gustaf and Queen Silvia
of Sweden

MENU

Fresh Asparagus
orange vinaigrette

Medallions of Lamb
green peppercorns

Mélange of Vegetables

Cheesecake
raspberry purée

Coffee
Tea

Great Western 1986 Special Selection Chardonnay
Great Western New York State Blanc de Blancs Champagne

This dinner was an unqualified success.

Another beautiful formal dinner was given in honor of the crew of the Challenger spacecraft. I am sure the astronauts would have welcomed even our least inspired efforts, after eating space "food," but we nevertheless went all out. They were served:

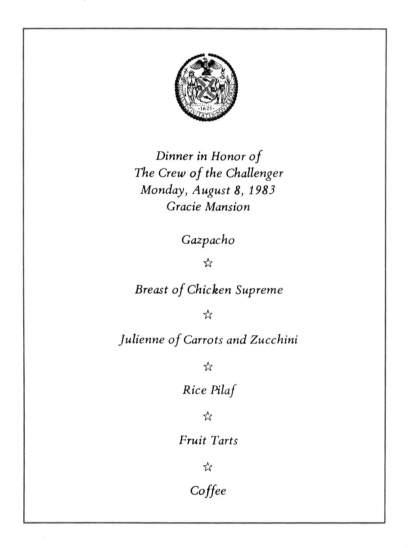

Dinner in Honor of
The Crew of the Challenger
Monday, August 8, 1983
Gracie Mansion

Gazpacho

☆

Breast of Chicken Supreme

☆

Julienne of Carrots and Zucchini

☆

Rice Pilaf

☆

Fruit Tarts

☆

Coffee

To come closest to the chicken supreme recipe, try our recipe for Chicken Breasts Stuffed with Duxelles (see Index).

I have cooked for many interesting people at Gracie Mansion, and naturally, there are a few I particularly enjoyed feeding. Henry Stern, the parks commissioner, is a delightful man who enjoyed my cooking—especially desserts. Fortunately, he never puts on an extra pound. Former Corporation Counsel Allen G. Schwartz was another appreciative guest for whom I enjoyed cooking.

Former New York State Assembly Speaker Stanley Fink often asked me for a recipe after he dined with the Mayor. I tried to have one typed up for him even before I served him dinner and to give it to him to take home.

One Chanukah dinner the Mayor had General Ariel Sharon of Israel and his wife as guests. Mrs. Sharon looked around and asked, "Where is the menorah?" (the special candelabrum lit for the holiday). The Mayor called me over and asked, "Where is the menorah?" I should have had one available, and I was embarrassed at my lapse. I brought one over, and Mrs. Sharon lit the candles. She sang the Hebrew blessings along with the general and his bodyguard.

Mayor Shlomo Lahat of Tel Aviv was also a guest at Gracie Mansion. I prepared, at his request, a typical Israeli breakfast of cubed cucumbers, tomatoes, and sour cream.

The famous opera star Sherrill Milnes did a program called "Live from Gracie Mansion." I had assumed that he wouldn't be eating dinner before his performance, but I was wrong. He dined on shrimp, steak, cheesecake, and cookies. It was only after I served this meal that I learned that certain singers prefer to sing on a full stomach. He is a full-stomach singer.

I think opera stars liked our food. After one dinner party, Luciano Pavarotti accepted the Mayor's invitation to put some cookies in his pocket for the road.

On Tuesday mornings, the Mayor often breakfasted with his cabinet—his commissioners and close advisers. I served this group hearty breakfasts, but the Mayor always had fruit.

Everyone makes mistakes, and to paraphrase a famous resident of Gracie Mansion, I have made some beauts in the course of my career. When I was abashed by a mistake, I usually announced it to the Mayor in the third person, which helped to diffuse the situation. For instance, one summer evening, I left a basic ingredient out of my Grand Marnier soufflé. I said, "The chef forgot to put the sugar in the soufflé."

Similarly, having iced a cake with the wrong chocolate, I announced, "The chef unfortunately iced the cake with unsweetened chocolate."

On another occasion I announced, "The chef forgot to light the grill. Dinner will be a little late." (Actually, I made this mistake a few times.)

To this, the Mayor replied (in jest), "Tell the chef to see how quickly he can pack!"

Because the Mayor appreciates good food, he understands that certain dishes won't wait, no matter how involved the guests may be in conversation. I always enjoyed cooking for him, because he was understanding and accommodating when food was ready somewhat before the guests were ready to eat it. When that happened, he simply stated, "The chef says we have to sit." This is a gracious way to interrupt people, and they usually didn't mind at all.

The Mayor knows his kitchen in great detail; in fact, he often knew better than I what we had in stock. This was not helpful in his dieting. He would ask: "Do we have any ice cream?" and I would answer, untruthfully but helpfully, "I don't know." "I know we have it," he would reply.

I often served the Mayor lighter food, while I gave guests somewhat richer fare. One night I presented him with Pureed Mussel Soup (an especially light dish, see Index) and the rest of the table with Mushroom Soup (see Index). I had neglected to tell him in advance, and since the soups looked alike, he assumed they were the same. He told his guests they were enjoying mussel soup, too. He was so convincing that most of them agreed, and the consensus was that it was a great mussel soup, if unusual.

I worked at Gracie Mansion seven years, and my job became more diverse with time and was always challenging and fascinating. But seven years, after all, is longer than many mayors remained at the Mansion—in fact, it was about one-fifth of my entire life. So in late 1988 I decided to move on.

My experience as a chef at Gracie Mansion could never be duplicated. First of all, I was fortunate enough to work for a unique boss, Mayor Ed Koch, for whom I had and have the greatest respect. In addition, I had a superb staff supporting me, and I was given complete responsibility for a complicated culinary and administrative operation.

As I have tried to indicate in the preceding pages, the Mansion was a fascinating and exciting place in which to work. I met many different people and became aware of the various aspects of New York life. It was an easy step from Gracie Mansion out into the world, with these rich seven years behind me.

A chef today finds many doors open to him. He can work happily in hotels, restaurants, private homes, in the travel industry, and in government, as well as in his own private enterprises. He can do what he likes best, travel, and make an excellent living. I have never regretted my early decision to cook professionally, because it has provided me with a rich, full life. And of that life so far, the best one-fifth has been spent at Gracie Mansion.

PART 1
BASICS

Methods

In this section I write about some of the basic methods that a cook uses in food preparation: broiling, grilling, roasting, steaming, poaching, sautéing, braising, blanching, and marinating. I have tried to give an overview of all these procedures and to explain my particular slant on each—how and when I use it, which method I may prefer for a particular food, how you can use the method most successfully.

But even after giving you all this information, I must stress that your common sense is paramount. If I tell you to grill a fish or vegetable, and you would prefer to roast it, you can easily make the transition from one method to another. As I explain, for both methods you use high, dry, heat; place food a certain distance from the source of heat depending upon its thickness; and test for doneness by seeing how the piece of food feels when you press it. Once you understand these cooking methods, it is up to you to experiment and change the directions I give you, depending upon what you want.

Your creativity and good judgment will give the recipes in this book your own particular stamp. Here are the rules, but don't hesitate to improvise:

BROILING

Broiling is one of the most healthful methods of preparing meats, fish, poultry, and even vegetables. There are two main reasons for this: when you broil food you use very little oil or butter, and broiling is fast, so it preserves nutrients. A bonus for the cook is the very small amount of time spent actually cooking.

Food is broiled when it is directly exposed to intense, dry heat. In broiling, the first and most important rule is that the broiler must be extremely hot. If it is not hot enough, you will not sear in the juices and flavors of the food.

Good results are impossible without this intense heat. I advise preheating the broiler thoroughly: at least 15 and up to 25 minutes. The home cook's usual 10 minutes' preheating is never long enough to get the broiler really hot. Remember: after preheating your broiler adequately, you will be cooking food for only about 4 minutes. (This preheating time is not optional and it is not wasteful of energy; your actual cooking time will be remarkably short in a properly heated broiler.)

One reason broiling worked so well for me at Gracie Mansion is that once the broiler is preheated, you can cook a good main course for four people in minutes. But broiled food will not wait for you once it is ready. You have to wait for it and then serve it immediately. Try some variation of Mayor Koch's "The chef says we have to sit down," if your guests seem otherwise occupied.

Foods that lend themselves to broiling are steaks, lamb and veal chops, and chicken. Whole fish are excellent for broiling, as are fish steaks and fillets. Fish rich in natural oils, such as salmon or bluefish, are ideally suited to broiling.

When broiling meats, chicken, or fish, I prefer to brush them with a combination of olive oil and a little butter: olive oil imparts flavor, and butter helps in browning the surface of the food. As with all my recipes, a little butter goes a long way and makes a difference in the finished product. Lemon butter is delicious on all varieties of fish:

2 tablespoons butter, melted
Juice of ½ lemon
2–3 grinds black pepper
2 teaspoons fresh tarragon, thyme, or parsley (or 1 teaspoon dried)

Combine all ingredients and brush fish before, during, and after broiling.

Light olive oil also works very well, adding a special emphasis to the more strongly flavored fish, such as bluefish. For a combination, try:

2 tablespoons olive oil
2 tablespoons butter, melted
Juice of ½ lemon
2 teaspoons fresh tarragon, thyme, or parsley (or 1 teaspoon dried)

Brush the food with this mixture before, during, and after broiling.

I often marinate swordfish, tuna, salmon, or shrimp, using the following for four portions:

❧❧ Marinade for Fish and Shrimp

¼ cup olive oil
Juice of 1 lemon
1 clove garlic, peeled and crushed
2 sprigs fresh thyme
Freshly ground black pepper

Marinate the fish 20 minutes. Brush with the marinade during broiling. Although this marinade contains ¼ cup of oil, most of that oil is not consumed. After broiling, discard whatever marinade remains.

Place your food about one inch from the source of heat if it is thin, and about two to three inches from the heat if it is thick (for instance, a two-inch-thick steak should be two to four inches from the heat.) Your object is to cook the food through without burning it. A thick steak has to be placed farther from the source of heat than a thin one, so that it won't burn on the outside before it is cooked on the inside. A thin fillet of fish can be placed very near the heat and will cook through quickly without even being turned.

Length of broiling time also depends upon the thickness of the food being broiled. The best test for doneness is simply to press the meat or fish in the center. If it is firm to the touch, it is cooked. If it is very soft, it is very rare.

Degree of doneness depends upon the taste of the individual guest, but this really presents no difficulty to the cook who is serving several different guests. The difference in cooking time between rare and well done is very small.

With fish, doneness can sometimes be tricky to gauge. The last thing you want is overdone, dried-out fish. Bluefish, which is strongly flavored and oily, should be cooked thoroughly. Salmon, on the other hand, being a delicate fish, can be served barely cooked. Cooked fish should feel firm when you press it, but not hard.

You must be very careful, in broiling, that your food does not dry out. You can avoid this misfortune by using thick cuts of meat and fish: meat should be 1¼ to 1½ inches thick; fish steaks should be 1 to 1½ inches thick. If you do broil thin slices of food, such as fish fillets of ¼-inch thickness, broil for only 2 minutes. (Remember that your broiler is very hot.)

GRILLING

There is something very cheerful and welcoming about a blazing fire in an outdoor grill. It adds a note of festive expectation to a dinner party. Sitting and enjoying drinks and hors d'oeuvres while the fire is prepared and then actually watching the food being grilled, guests find their enjoyment of the main course is increased. The wonderful aromas coming from the grill add to this.

Grilling is similar to broiling, in that it uses very high, dry heat. As I mentioned earlier, in warm weather I enjoyed cooking outdoors on a large grill. The kitchen in Gracie Mansion has an excellent, large indoor grill. But for the average home, a standard barbecue grill is more than adequate. In the recipes that require a fire, you may use either charcoal or wood—they are really interchangeable.

We grilled food for years at Gracie Mansion—we started long before California chic made its way into New York's restaurants. Not only did we grill meat and fish, we also prepared vegetables on our barbecues. We even served Grilled Pizza (see Index), which we grilled first and then baked.

In grilling, as in broiling, thin slices cook faster than thick. Thinner foods should be placed close to the fire, where they will cook through quickly and not dry out. For instance, a ¼-inch-thick fillet of sole should be placed approximately 1 inch from the heat. Thicker slices of meat or fish should be farther from the heat so that they have a chance to cook thoroughly without burning: a 1-inch-thick halibut steak should be placed about 3–4 inches from the fire.

Good foods for grilling are sirloin, shellfish, and fillet steaks; rib and loin veal chops; rib and loin lamb chops; whole fish, fish fillets, and fish steaks; and vegetables.

To grill steaks, first grind black pepper over the meat, then salt it lightly. I find light salting enhances the flavor and does not affect the food's juiciness, since the high heat of the grill sears in the meat's juices. Place the steak 3–4 inches from the heat and brush with oil or oil and butter, as described in the broiling section. Turn the steak twice during grilling, brushing each time. A well-grilled piece of meat will be charred on the outside and slightly underdone inside.

Grill lamb and veal chops in the same manner.

I like to marinate veal chops in the following marinade (for four chops, 1½ inches thick):

⚜⚜⚜ Veal Chop Marinade

½ cup olive oil
¼ cup fresh rosemary leaves
2 cloves garlic, peeled and crushed
Juice of 1 lemon

Marinate the chops 20-30 minutes. Brush with the marinade twice during cooking. To avoid consuming extra calories, you can pat the veal dry before you grill it. Discard any extra marinade after grilling the meat. Be especially careful not to overcook veal—it cooks the fastest of all the meats.

For all foods, grilling time will depend upon thickness, the heat of the fire, and the number of pieces you are grilling. As with broiling, test for doneness by pressing the meat or fish in the center. If it is firm and resistant to your touch, it is done. Vegetables are done when they are slightly limp and have turned golden brown.

The technique for grilling fish is slightly different from that for meat. Again, you can grill whole fish, steaks, or fillets. The main problem in grilling fish is that the fish skin sticks to the metal grill. After many years of preparing fish, I found a good way to avoid this problem. Before placing a fillet on the grill, brush it with oil, with butter and oil, or with butter (see recipes in the broiling section) on the meat side first—not the skin side. Put it on the grill meat side down. When it is firm, turn, brush, and grill on the skin side. At this point, it should not stick. You need to turn the fish only once. If you turn more than once, you have done something wrong. If you are grilling a fish steak, then, of course, you have two meat sides, and you avoid any problems with sticking because of the skin.

When you grill a whole fish, brush it with oil or butter and oil and place it approximately 4-5 inches from the fire. You must take extra care in turning the fish to avoid the skin's sticking to the grill. After the fish has browned well, move it away from the center of the heat so it can continue to cook without burning.

Vegetables are delicious prepared on a barbecue grill. Good vegetables for grilling are zucchini, yellow summer squash, eggplant, tomatoes, and yellow and red peppers. Cut them as follows:

zucchini, yellow squash: cut lengthwise or into rounds, about ⅓ inch
   thick
eggplant: cut into rounds about ½ inch thick
tomatoes: cut into halves
peppers: cut into halves

Slice the vegetables thick enough so that they do not fall through the grill
onto the fire. Just to be sure, you can place a second grill rack crosswise
over the first.

Drizzle the vegetables with olive oil and sprinkle them lightly with salt
and pepper. The vegetables will be somewhat charred when finished, with
a wonderful texture and aroma. This preparation is the simplest of the
simple and the best of the best.

ROASTING

Food is roasted when it is cooked uncovered in an oven in high, dry heat.
The most important thing to remember when roasting is to use a high
initial temperature, from 425°F to 475°F. This is true whether you roast
beef, lamb, veal, chicken, or turkey. The high temperature sears the food
and locks in the flavor. After the food has been seared, do not continue
cooking at the initial temperature. Turn down the heat and roast until
done.

How far you turn down the temperature depends upon what you are
roasting. Start a turkey at 450°F and turn it down to 350°F. It should
continue cooking at this lower temperature because it is a large bird and
needs enough time to cook through without burning on the outside. When
you roast a chicken, which is considerably smaller than a turkey, start it at
450°F and turn it down to 400°F after it has been seared. It will not take
long to cook through.

It is also very important that you do not cover the food. I know this is
contrary to grandmother's recipes, but it is vital. Whenever you cover food,
you are steaming it, not roasting it.

Some of my favorite foods are roasted. About three times a year I cook a
special treat for myself: a perfectly Roasted Chicken with Black Peppercorns. I especially enjoy this with a Caesar Salad. The recipe is simplicity
itself (see Index).

When roasting a whole fish, try stuffing it with fresh herbs and some
whole fennel, as I do for Roasted Striped Bass with Roasted Fennel (see
Index).

STEAMING

Roasting and grilling use dry heat, while steaming is the opposite, in that it uses moist heat. It is a very healthful method of preparing food, because you can cut out fats entirely. You still get wonderful results in terms of flavor, texture, and color. Properly steamed vegetables are crisp, juicy, colorful, and flavorful. In addition, they retain their important nutrients.

In steaming, herbs can make the difference between boring and interesting food. You are not adding the flavor of butter or oil to your food, and you need a replacement. Fresh, fragrant herbs are ideal and easy to find all year round.

You do not need any special equipment to steam food. I often use a large pot into which I put just enough water to cover the bottom. I cook vegetables by bringing this film of water to a boil and putting the food directly into the pot. The small amount of water soon becomes steam and quickly cooks the vegetables.

If you prefer, you can use a steamer basket or insert that fits into a large pot and holds the food above the boiling water. You can also steam shrimp or scallops in a colander over boiling water (about 2 to 3 inches) in a large pot.

Clams can be steamed in a very small amount of water and then mixed with herbs and other flavorings. You can also steam shrimp and vegetables together for an excellent one-dish meal. Try Steamed Littleneck Clams with Garlic and Parsley or Steamed Shrimp with Ginger (see Index).

POACHING

Poaching is similar to steaming, in that it, too, is a moist rather than a dry method of cooking. In poaching, food is cooked very slowly in a simmering liquid. If you expect the finished product to taste like anything, don't simmer in plain water. You will get far better results if you use a court bouillon (a seasoned broth with vegetables), which takes only 20 minutes to prepare. Or poach in a fish stock, made with fish bones, wine, vegetables, and herbs, which can be made in 30 minutes. Chicken and veal stocks take somewhat longer to prepare, but they can be frozen and then defrosted when you need to use them. They are wonderful poaching liquids and well worth the small effort it takes to make them. You will find recipes for them in the section on stocks.

Fish and shellfish are excellent foods to poach. Chicken can be poached, too, although I find roasted chicken much more delicious. However, for an excellent, tasty light meal try poached chicken surrounded by a bouquet of steamed vegetables, such as carrots, onions, and green beans. Beef can be poached, and I include a recipe for Poached Fillet of Beef (see Index). A mixture of Roasted Vegetables (see Index) makes a colorful low-fat accompaniment. Add Horseradish Sauce (see Index) for a little zip, and you have an interesting, filling meal. Although this is not my favorite way of preparing beef, I urge you to try it—it is really quite good.

To poach food, bring to a simmer enough court bouillon or stock to cover. Add fresh herbs and the food to be poached. Keep the poaching liquid at a simmer throughout the cooking time.

If you are poaching fish, don't cook any other food in the stock with the fish. Use no fat at all and skim the broth frequently. The exquisite flavor of fresh fish is highlighted when the fish is carefully poached—plus you have the benefit of a low-fat dish.

Good, flavorful fish to poach whole are salmon and striped bass. A 3-4 pound fish should take about 15-20 minutes' poaching time. Light Tomato Sauce (see Index) goes well with all these fish dishes.

SAUTEING

To sauté food, brown it in very hot fat in a frying pan, shaking the pan and/or turning the food to brown all surfaces. Sautéing cooks food quickly, browns it beautifully, and imparts a delicious flavor.

Although sautéing provides very tasty food, it is not the most healthful method of preparation, since it requires fat. However, you can use as little fat as possible. Just cover the pan with a film of olive oil and add a little butter for flavor. When you are cooking a dish containing tomatoes and garlic, use olive oil alone, although I do feel that certain dishes require butter for sautéing.

I don't like to use nonstick pans, even though they require little or no fat, because you cannot heat them to a high enough temperature to properly brown and cook the food.

You can sauté a meal for two in just 2 tablespoons of oil or oil combined with butter. I love a meal of sautéed veal scallops accompanied by roasted vegetables and perhaps preceded by a light dish of angel hair pasta. There is nothing wrong with that after a hard day.

Very few foods cannot be sautéed. The method works well for veal, chicken, fish, steak, potatoes, onions, cherry tomatoes—just use your imagination.

To prepare food for sautéing, cut it into reasonably equal pieces and dry it carefully. In some cases, dust lightly with flour. In a heavy pan large enough to accommodate the food, heat the oil or oil and butter until it is very hot (if you can smell it, it is on the verge of burning). The food must not be crowded in the pan, or it will steam rather than brown.

Strictly speaking, you should keep the food moving while it cooks. However, I would not sacrifice the rest of the dinner for the food in the sauté pan. You must turn the food, but you can leave the pan and take care of the other things you are cooking at the same time. This way you can have all elements of your main course ready together.

Although this sounds most unorthodox, you can sauté with no fat at all when you pan-fry steak. Preheat a heavy cast-iron pan for 6–7 minutes, or until it is very hot. The steak will brown beautifully in this pan.

When you sauté chicken pieces, be sure to start the legs and thighs first. When they have browned, add the white parts of the chicken. When all pieces are browned, turn down the heat and continue cooking.

Sautéing fish requires care and delicacy. For scallops of salmon, start with a fillet. Place the fish skin side down on a cutting surface. Slice thin diagonal scallops, about ¼ inch thick, holding the knife almost horizontal to the fish. These thin scallops will cook in seconds in hot olive oil or oil and butter, or they can be quickly broiled. They are delicious accompanied by Steamed Haricots Verts (see Index).

BRAISING

When food is braising in your kitchen, the room is perfumed with the subtle and inviting essences of onion, garlic, stock, and spices. Braised foods are first browned, then cooked with liquid in a covered pot. Braising is a long, slow cooking process using moist heat.

I don't give many recipes for braised foods in this book, not because I don't enjoy them, but because we are aiming for quickness of preparation. Some dishes that I do include are Pot Roast of Veal with Pearl Onions, Osso Buco, and Braised Fennel (see Index).

BLANCHING

Blanching is cooking food very briefly in boiling water. The food is not completely cooked when it is blanched; it is just prepared for whatever will come next. You blanch tomatoes, for example, simply to loosen the skin so that they can be peeled easily. It isn't necessary to heat a large pot full of water for blanching. Just a little boiling water to cover will suffice.

MARINATING

A marinade is a mixture of oil, wine or vinegar, herbs, and seasonings that tenderizes and flavors the food that is placed in it. In the Gracie Mansion kitchen, we used marinades mainly for meat and fish that we were going to grill or broil.

Your own common sense will guide you when you marinate food. Delicate fish and shellfish become permeated with their marinade quite quickly, so you need to marinate them for only 15–30 minutes. Leg of lamb and flank steak, on the other hand, are strong in flavor and texture. They require a marination time of 24–48 hours to fully benefit from the process.

After you remove meat or fish from its marinade, keep the marinade and use it to brush the food while it is cooking.

KITCHEN ESSENTIALS

I enjoyed having the Gracie Mansion kitchen to work in because it is an efficient, well-equipped space (I describe this kitchen in my introduction). The average home kitchen can serve just as well, providing you have the right equipment.

First of all, any serious cook needs a serious set of knives. You should have a 10-inch cook's knife, a paring knife, and a serrated knife for bread and tomatoes—of carbon or stainless steel. You also will need a sharpening steel to keep these knives functioning well.

The pans you use should be heavy and of very high quality. I prefer copper that is lined with stainless steel, or Calphalon. These are very good for sautéing, frying, and browning. I do not use Teflon-lined pans because you cannot heat them high enough to really brown food. Avoid aluminum-lined pans; they impart a metallic taste to food. I generally use sauté pans that are 8 and 10 inches in diameter.

Make sure that any pan or pot you use is large enough to accommodate food comfortably so that you can handle what you are cooking. Nothing is more aggravating than trying to cook in a pot that is too small. However, please don't go to the opposite extreme and cook everything in an extra-large pot.

For mixing your simmering food, you will need heavy-duty wooden spoons, which you can find at restaurant supply stores. You will also find a thin, piano-wire whisk to be very useful for the recipes in this book.

I use a food processor for purees, and I also use a food mill for recipes such as Dinner-in-Itself Fish Soup (see Index). The processor purees everything you place in it, and sometimes this is not what you want. The food mill allows you to extract the flavor of fish and leave the bones behind. Be sure to use a heavy-duty professional food mill that will not bend or break.

I much prefer gas stoves and ovens over electric. Gas allows you to regulate heat and provides higher temperatures than electric elements. For grilling, you need not be so fussy. In Provence, I have grilled beautiful meals using a heavy wire rack set over bricks, just like the Boy Scouts do. It is important that your fire be adequate and that you allow it to burn down to embers before you cook your food.

Vegetables and Herbs in Food Preparation

Light Tomato Sauce

Roasted Shiitake Mushrooms

Duxelles

Roasted Peppers

Roasted Garlic

Horseradish Sauce

Bouquet Garni

Pesto

Pasta with Pesto

Light Pesto Sauce

Yogurt and Basil Sauce

Mint Lemonade

Persillade

Yogurt and Parsley Sauce

Since this is a commonsense cookbook, the few rules I give you are down to earth and easy to follow. I have nothing esoteric to tell you about setting your table and feeding your guests and family, and I do not believe in dressing up vegetables so that they are hardly recognizable. I will not teach you to flute mushroom caps or wrap leeks around bundles of other leeks.

I believe there is no better gastronomic treat than vegetables and fruits in their glorious prime. You have only to buy the best your market has to offer and to serve it simply.

I cannot stress this last point strongly enough. I am very impatient with most of those overly fussy artistic arrangements of vegetables or salads so popular today. They make me wonder how many hands spent how many minutes handling the food I am expected to eat. Vegetables are vegetables, beautiful in themselves, and art is art. I don't like to confuse the two.

Use your good judgment in purchasing vegetables and follow the seasons. Most produce is available year round (the same is true for fish and shellfish), but it is worth buying only in its season. Tomatoes bought in winter are mealy, and zucchini tastes bitter. But winter vegetables like turnips, parsnips, and sweet potatoes are appropriately filling and satisfying. Spring and summer are truly worth waiting for, to give yourself the experience of enjoying nature's best.

Many areas are lucky enough to have greenmarkets and farm stands operating during the summer. I took a guest of mine, a chef from Switzerland, to the Union Square green market in Manhattan and he was amazed at the quality and availability of our strawberries, zucchini, peaches, and corn, to name just a few of the fruits and vegetables there.

In New York I have found some of my favorite seasonal herbs and vegetables are at their best at the following times:

artichokes: March through June
asparagus: April through June
basil: May through September

cauliflower: fall and winter
corn (yellow): July through September
corn (white): August, September
fennel: October through March
leeks: October through March
wild mushrooms (morels, chanterelles, cepes, porcini, shiitake):
   September through January
red and yellow peppers: April through November
sorrel: May through September
tomatoes (red): August, September
tomatoes (yellow): August
zucchini: July, August

TOMATOES

Choose red (or yellow), firm tomatoes that smell fresh. By firm, I do not mean hard as a rock. Hard tomatoes are simply underripe. I like to buy half of my tomatoes just right for serving and half a bit too hard. These I ripen on a rack in the sun. They are delicious, especially served at room temperature.

To peel and seed tomatoes: Boil enough water to cover tomatoes. Place tomatoes in boiling water 10 seconds. The skin will break. Remove from water. Cut each tomato in half. Cut out core. Gently squeeze out the seeds. You now have a tomato concasse. It is ready for use in many recipes, such as soups, sauces, and salads.

❧ Light Tomato Sauce

This is a good light sauce to serve with roasted or grilled fish. Place it on the side of the platter or individual plate as a garnish.

6   tomatoes, peeled and seeded
2   tablespoons olive oil
2   cloves garlic, peeled (optional)
Salt and freshly ground black pepper
¼   cup fresh tarragon and basil (optional)
2   teaspoons fresh thyme (*or* ¼ teaspoon dried, optional)

1. Cut tomatoes into large dice.

2. Heat olive oil in sauté pan and sauté tomatoes and garlic, if desired, over high heat 3 minutes.

3. Remove from heat. Season with salt and pepper to taste. Add herbs, if desired.

Makes 2 cups

MUSHROOMS

We often served wild mushrooms at Gracie Mansion. Mainly we used shiitake, which are good served on their own as a first course. I like to roast them with garlic and thyme. Chanterelles and morels were also favorites, although I found that these mushrooms are better served with something, such as pasta or veal.

❧ Roasted Shiitake Mushrooms

2   tablespoons olive oil
1   pound shiitake mushrooms, caps only
10   cloves garlic, with skin, slightly mashed
6-8   sprigs fresh thyme
Salt and freshly ground black pepper

1. Heat oven to 400°F.

2. Heat oil in frying pan. Add mushroom caps and toss over high heat. Add garlic and thyme. Season with salt and pepper to taste.

3. Roast in oven 15-20 minutes until soft, with crisp edges.

Makes 4 portions

Mushrooms (domestic are fine) that are chopped and sautéed until dry are called duxelles. This mixture is used to give a pronounced mushroom flavor to soup, sauce, veal, and fish, as in Steamed Fillet of Sole with Duxelles, Wrapped in Spinach (see Index). Duxelles is best made fresh or used within three days. It is easy to do, so make what you need when you need it.

⚜ Duxelles

2   tablespoons butter
1   cup peeled, chopped shallots
3   pounds domestic mushrooms, washed quickly in cold water and
     chopped fine (do not use food processor)

1. Melt butter in a heavy pan. Add shallots and cook 30 seconds.

2. Add mushrooms. Stir and cook over high heat until all the
moisture has evaporated.

Makes 3 cups

PEPPERS

Roasted peppers make a wonderful hors d'oeuvre or addition to a salad.
Always roast sweet red or yellow peppers; green peppers are too bitter for
roasting. Peppers are best roasted over a wood fire, but a gas burner will
do. If you don't have a gas stove, then use a broiler or a barbecue.

Some cooks complicate the process of roasting peppers by adding an
unnecessary step. After removing the peppers from the fire, they place
them in a paper bag to "steam," before removing the skin. Don't bother—
this will do nothing for your peppers.

⚜ Roasted Peppers

6   red peppers or a combination of red and yellow peppers

1. Roast each pepper directly over the gas flame, turning, until
blackened on all sides. When skin is blackened, remove pepper from flame,
slice in half, and remove seeds.

2. Holding peppers under cold, running water, scrape away the
blackened skin with a knife blade.

Makes 6 roasted peppers

Cut the peppers into julienne if desired and combine with the dressing of your choice, as in the appetizer Roasted Red and Yellow Peppers (see Index). You can also use roasted peppers in such recipes as Fettuccine with Goat Cheese, Basil, and Red Peppers; Veal Chops with Red and Yellow Peppers; and Steamed Scallops in Spinach Leaves, on a Bed of Roasted Peppers (see Index).

ONIONS

In the meals I prepared for Mayor Koch, I often served him vidalia onions, a sweet variety available in the spring. For stocks and soups, I generally used Spanish onions. Bermuda onions were served raw with smoked salmon—a wonderful combination. I found pearl onions hard to work with, but I have included one recipe calling for them—Pot Roast of Veal with Pearl Onions (see Index)—and it is delicious. Pearl onions are easier to peel if you first plunge them briefly into boiling water.

GARLIC

In my years at Gracie Mansion I came to appreciate garlic and to use it liberally. No, I did not prepare garlic and strawberries, as has been reported. However, I did combine it with many foods, and I had excellent results. I understand that medical researchers are studying garlic's use as a possible aid to cholesterol control. And I believe the legend that garlic adds to longevity and sharpens mental powers. I am sure Mayor Koch will concur.

As I noted earlier, Provence has exerted a strong influence on my cooking. When one cooks Provençale style, garlic and fresh herbs perfume and enrich many dishes.

Garlic adds spirit to food. Raw garlic has the strongest flavor; once it is cooked, garlic becomes milder. I don't believe in hiding its flavor, as some cooks advise. I use it liberally in such recipes as Roast Leg of Lamb, Dinner-in-Itself Fish Soup, Osso Buco, salads, and hors d'oeuvres (see Index). Garlic is easier to peel if you crush the clove slightly first.

It is easy to buy fresh garlic; there is no season when it is not available in supermarkets and local shops. It is at its best when it is fresh; the cloves should not be mushy or sprouted.

When roasted, garlic is sweet and delicious and makes an excellent accompaniment to grilled meats, fish, and poultry. It also combines well with roasted eggplant in Eggplant Puree (see Index).

♣ Roasted Garlic

1 head of garlic
½ teaspoon olive oil

Preheat oven to 350°F. Slightly open 1 head of garlic, leaving it together at the base and leaving the cloves in the skin. Sprinkle with olive oil. Roast 30 minutes. When done, scoop the garlic out of its crisp skin to eat.

Makes 1 portion

SHALLOTS

Shallots are a combination of onions and garlic, with all the good qualities of both and none of the harshness of either. They are considerably more subtle and expensive than either onions or garlic and are not used in quantity. They give a little extra flavor to a dish but do not overpower it.

HORSERADISH

Freshly grated horseradish root is a piquant addition to sauces. It goes well with beef, vegetables, and seafood. Fresh horseradish is available at most supermarkets and vegetable markets, so it is easy to avoid the bottled version.

♣ Horseradish Sauce

This zesty sauce is delicious with poached fillet of beef and roasted or steamed vegetables.

2 cups plain low-fat or nonfat yogurt
4 tablespoons ground fresh horseradish
Pinch each of salt and white pepper
Dash Tabasco sauce

Combine all ingredients.

Makes 2 cups

HERBS

The herb garden at Gracie Mansion included lush plantings of basil, tarragon, oregano, chives, dill, chervil, rosemary, lemon thyme, thyme, mint, peppermint, and both curly and flat-leaf parsley. It is rare in Manhattan to be able to walk out to your backyard and pick herbs for three hundred people, and I consider myself to have been lucky.

Even when the garden was snowed under, I had no problem finding herbs at local markets. Fresh herbs are available almost everywhere and are a real boon to the cook. I use herbs in many dishes and often mix and match as the herbs themselves move me.

Bouquet Garni

A bouquet garni of fresh herbs is indispensable when you are braising dishes or making sauces or soups.

4   sprigs parsley
1   bay leaf
1   tablespoon peppercorns
4   sprigs fresh thyme (*or* ½ tablespoon dried)

Tie herbs in a bag of washed cheesecloth and place in the simmering liquid.

Here are some other, general uses for my favorite herbs. These reflect my personal tastes and prejudices; use your imagination in finding other ways to use them:

Basil

Basil is a natural partner for garlic, as proved by the success of pesto. A little pesto enlivens almost any food. I like to use it on pizzas and fish, as well as in pasta.

Basil alone enhances fish, soups, and salads. It goes especially well with ripe tomatoes.

⚜⚜⚜ Pesto

This garlicky, aromatic sauce is a summer favorite. It is delicious on pasta, tomato salads, pizzas, and fish.

4   cups fresh basil leaves, washed
4   cloves garlic, peeled
½   cup grated Parmesan
¼   cup shelled walnuts or pignoli
1   cup olive oil

   1.   Roughly puree all ingredients in a food processor.
   2.   To store in the refrigerator, film the top with olive oil and wrap tightly. You can freeze pesto if you omit the cheese; after freezing stir in cheese when ready to use.

Makes 1½ cups

⚜⚜⚜ Pasta with Pesto

4   quarts water
2   teaspoons salt
2   tablespoons oil
1   pound angel hair pasta
¾   cup Pesto (see Index)
Salt and freshly ground black pepper (optional)

   1.   Bring water to a boil in a large pot. Add 2 teaspoons salt and oil. Add pasta and boil until done to taste. Drain.
   2.   Mix 3 tablespoons water from the pasta pot into the Pesto. (Pesto as is will be dry.) Combine Pesto and pasta. Season with salt and pepper, if desired.

Makes 4 portions

❧❧❧ Light Pesto Sauce

¾ cup Pesto (see Index)
6 tablespoons water (*or* chicken broth)

When you add approximately ¾ cup of Pesto to pasta, you generally mix it with 3 tablespoons of hot water from the pasta pot to improve its consistency. Add another 3 tablespoons water or chicken broth, and you have a light pesto sauce.

Makes ¾ cup

Basil combines well with yogurt and garlic to make a delicious sauce for crudités.

❧ Yogurt and Basil Sauce

1   cup plain low-fat or nonfat yogurt
½   bunch basil, chopped fine
1–3 cloves garlic, peeled and minced

Combine all ingredients.

Makes 1½ cups

Chervil

Chervil is a delicate herb resembling parsley. It is delicious on fish or with asparagus, hot or cold. It also adds flavor to a vinaigrette (see Index for recipe for Chervil Vinaigrette).

Chives

Chives are delicious in a cool yogurt sauce. I also use them with tomatoes and in tomato sauce. I like them with fish and salads, but not with beef or lamb.

Dill

Dill doesn't see much use in my kitchen. I just don't like it as much as some other herbs—this is a matter of personal taste. I sometimes add dill to a yogurt sauce, but that's about it.

Fennel

Although fennel is a vegetable, and a favorite ingredient in my salads and cooked dishes, its feathery leaves are used as herbs. They are delicious with roasted or grilled fish and in soups.

Mint

Mint and peppermint are interchangeable in our famous fresh lemonade.

⚜ Mint Lemonade

2 cups sugar
About 1 quart water
Juice of 4 medium lemons
1 sprig of mint or peppermint per glass
Ice cubes

1. Make simple syrup: combine 2 cups sugar and 1 cup water. Boil 5 minutes. Makes 2 cups syrup.
2. Combine juice of lemons and ¼ cup of the cooled syrup in a pitcher. Add water to make 1 quart. Add mint and ice cubes to individual glasses.

Makes 1 quart

A very little bit of mint added to seafood dishes (hot or cold) is a great flavor enhancer.

Oregano

Oregano is a forceful herb that is delicious with pizza, pasta, fish, and chicken. It goes well with tomato sauces.

Parsley

Parsley simply goes with everything. I prefer the flat-leaf or Italian variety to the curly leaf, but I use both in abundance. It is more than the garnish so many people consider it to be. I like it with fish, lamb, poultry, vegetables—almost everything except dessert.

⚜ Persillade

Persillade is a simple mixture of chopped parsley and garlic that does wonderful things for lamb, fish, pizza, and grilled and roasted vegetables.

3 cloves garlic, peeled
1 bunch Italian parsley, quickly washed in cold water

Chop together the garlic and parsley finely. Use immediately or within 2 days.

Makes 1 cup

Here is a variation of the yogurt and basil sauce offered earlier. It is equally good.

⚜ Yogurt and Parsley Sauce

1 cup plain low-fat or nonfat yogurt
½ bunch Italian parsley, chopped fine
Dash Tabasco sauce

Combine all ingredients.

Makes 1½ cups

Peppercorns

Most of my recipes call for freshly ground peppercorns. However, coarsely crushed peppercorns are also useful. To crush peppercorns coarsely, sprinkle on a work surface. Place the flat blade of a knife over them and pound your hand back and forth over the blade.

Rosemary

Rosemary, with its strong flavor, is especially good with lamb or chicken.

Sorrel

Sorrel has a somewhat sour taste. It is usually cooked and is delicious in soups. A special favorite of Mayor Koch's is Poached Salmon with Sorrel Sauce (see Index).

Tarragon

Tarragon goes well with fish and veal. It imparts a special flavor to stuffing for fish, which can then be grilled, steamed, or poached.

Thyme

Thyme, both lemon and regular, adds a special accent to fish, pasta, and tomato sauces. It is delicious with lamb.

Stocks

Brown Veal Stock
Chicken Stock
Fish Stock or Fumet
Court Bouillon

The wonderful thing about many of my favorite recipes is that they can be prepared so efficiently and quickly. Yet they are delicious, and they have that special, elegant quality. I have a not-so-secret ingredient that ensures these perfect results, and I am happy to share it with you: stocks.

Stocks can be prepared in a short time and can be refrigerated or frozen. They definitely make the difference between ordinary and extraordinary dishes. You can prepare all the stock you will need for many meals in just a few hours and then freeze it for the future. I generally freeze extra stock in 1- or 2-cup containers, but you can even freeze stock in ice-cube molds and defrost just a small amount to enrich your sauce, soup, or sauté.

There is no reason to use a commercial product when you can prepare your own stocks so easily, using the freshest and best ingredients. The recipes in the following pages include a brown veal stock that can be used for veal, beef, and chicken-based dishes. I also give a chicken stock for vegetable- and chicken-based dishes and a fish stock or fumet, very quickly prepared, for cooking fish or shellfish. I include a Court Bouillon, also very quick, for fish, shellfish, and vegetable preparation.

If you continue to cook and reduce your stock, as I point out in the individual recipes, you will have a reduction, a very rich flavoring liquid that is excellent in sauces. But these days few people go to the trouble to make reductions. I prefer to make an excellent rich stock and freeze or refrigerate it. When I use this stock in a particular recipe, I can then reduce the small amount I need, or I can reduce it as part of the cooking procedure of that recipe. Nevertheless, I describe the technique for reducing stocks, in case you care to try it.

❧ Brown Veal Stock

This recipe is not intended to keep you in the kitchen for three days—or even for one day. Follow these steps, and you will have great success. This stock is light, since you remove all fat during cooking.

5   pounds veal bones (have your butcher split them)
1   pound veal shank or other inexpensive cut of meat
2   medium carrots, washed and cut into rounds
1   medium onion, peeled and sliced
4   quarts water
1   Bouquet Garni (see Index)

1.   Preheat oven to 400°F.

2.   Spread bones in a large roasting pan and roast until very well browned, about 30 minutes, turning once or twice. Add meat halfway through. Add vegetables and roast until browned. Do not burn anything, and if something does burn, discard it, or it will affect the entire batch of stock.

3.   Place bones, meat, and vegetables in a large pot and cover with the water. Bring to a simmer, being careful not to boil. Skim fat from top.

4.   Add Bouquet Garni and simmer 5-7 hours, skimming when needed. Strain and let cool to room temperature before refrigerating. The finished stock should be very brown and very clear.

Makes 3 quarts

Variation: Make a double batch and reserve half when finished. Continue simmering the remainder 2-3 hours. This reduced stock will make excellent sauces for both veal and beef dishes, and a little of it will go a long way. The original stock is suitable for soups and for braising.

❧ Chicken Stock

This simple stock is a must for any chicken-based soup. Backs and necks produce the most flavorful stock. Because you skim off all fat, this qualifies as light.

10 pounds chicken backs and necks, well washed
 7 quarts cold water
 8 medium carrots, washed and cut into rounds
 1 pound domestic mushrooms or mushroom stems, cleaned
 1 bunch parsley, stems only
 3 ribs celery, washed and sliced thin
 2 large leeks, washed very well and sliced thin, including the white and 1 inch of the green
 1 Bouquet Garni (see Index)

1. Place chicken parts in a large stockpot with the water and bring to a boil. Reduce to a simmer. Let simmer 10 minutes, skimming foam and fat from the top.

2. Add vegetables and Bouquet Garni. Simmer 3–4 hours, skimming occasionally.

3. Strain stock and let cool to room temperature. Refrigerate. When stock is cold, remove all fat from the top.

Makes 4 quarts stock

Variation: Make a double batch and reserve half when finished. Continue simmering the remainder 2–3 hours or until it is reduced by half. This will make a stronger stock for flavoring sauces.

❧ Fish Stock or Fumet

This is the simplest of all stocks to make, and it is indispensable for poaching fish and for sauces. Only flounder or sole bones and heads may be used—no other fish.

2 pounds flounder or sole fish bones (heads optional)
2 quarts cold water
1 cup white wine
3 medium carrots, scraped
2 large onions, peeled and julienned
¼ pound mushrooms, rinsed
1 Bouquet Garni (see Index)

   1. Rinse all fish bones and heads well.
   2. Place all ingredients in a large pot and bring to a simmer. Skim. Simmer 30 minutes and strain.

Makes 1 quart

⚜ Court Bouillon

A Court Bouillon is simply a seasoned broth consisting of water, white wine, herbs, and seasonings that is used to poach fish. It contributes flavor and aroma to the fish and is a much better poaching medium than plain water.

3 quarts water
2 cups dry white wine
1 lemon, cut into rounds
2 carrots, washed and cut into rounds
1 onion, peeled and sliced
1 bunch parsley stems
1 Bouquet Garni (see Index)

   1. Place all ingredients in a large pot and bring to a boil.
   2. Simmer 20 minutes and strain. The Court Bouillon is now ready to be used for poaching fish and seafood.

Makes 2½ quarts

PART 2
RECIPES

The recipes are rated as follows:

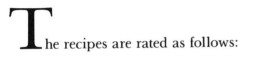 Light, containing little or no fat or sugar

Moderate, containing a small amount of fat or some sugar

Rich, containing larger amounts of fat or sugar

Appetizers

Roasted Red and Yellow Peppers

Asparagus with Parmesan

Tomatoes with Fresh Basil

Bruschetta alla Romana

Roasted Vegetables

Broiled Wild Mushrooms

Marinated Zucchini

Grilled Marinated Tomatoes with Basil

Grilled Eggplant and Tomatoes with Yogurt Sauce

Eggplant with Tomatoes

Grilled Salmon Chunks

Steamed Artichokes with Yogurt and Basil Sauce

Grilled Pizza

Appetizers are the first course you see in each meal, but in my kitchen, they are generally the last course to be planned. Planning which appetizer to serve requires not so much inspiration as common sense, because the appetizer, more than any other course, must suit the needs of the cook at a particular time and must fit in with the rest of the meal.

When I cooked in the Gracie Mansion kitchen, we were so tied to schedules that we had to do things on the quick side. What we served was governed not only by the time we had to prepare it but also by the number of guests we expected. I prefer hot appetizers: with few exceptions, food that is good cold will be better hot. But obviously it is difficult to do hot appetizers for one hundred people. So, for large parties, my favorite hot asparagus was translated into cold asparagus. (It was still terrific.)

An important consideration for the home chef, as well as for the professional, is that the appetizer blend with the main course and dessert. With a main course of Broiled Chicken, Grilled Eggplant and Tomatoes with Yogurt Sauce is an appropriate appetizer. At the same time, you don't want to duplicate ingredients or flavors, so you would not serve Roasted Vegetables before a pasta primavera. If the main course is somewhat rich, the appetizer must be especially simple; if the main course is simple, then you can splurge a little in your first course.

When I plan a main course of grilled salmon and a dessert of sorbet, I like hot Asparagus with Parmesan for a first course. If the party is large, as I said earlier, then it is easier for the chef if the asparagus is cold. Most vegetables, shellfish, and salads make good appetizers.

Ten or fifteen minutes seems to me the optimum time to spend eating the appetizer portion of the meal. This interlude sets the tone for what is to come in terms of both cuisine and conversation.

⚜⚜ Roasted Red and Yellow Peppers

This recipe must be made on a gas burner; an electric stove cannot be used. A barbecue gives even better results.

These peppers are both beautiful to look at and wonderful to eat. They proved successful with the Mayor's guests at Gracie Mansion and often were what you could find the chef eating in his own kitchen.

2 red peppers
2 yellow peppers
1 tablespoon balsamic vinegar
3 tablespoons olive oil
Pinch of salt

1. Put each whole pepper directly on a gas burner turned up high and roast until blackened, turning frequently.

2. Cut each pepper in half and remove seeds. Run under cold water and scrape with a knife blade to remove blackened skin.

3. Arrange peppers on platter, alternating red and yellow.

4. For dressing, combine vinegar, olive oil, and salt. Pour over peppers.

Makes 4 portions

❧❧ Asparagus with Parmesan

Freshly grated Parmesan is essential to this dish, as is freshly ground black pepper. There is no better way to eat asparagus.

1¼ pounds medium asparagus
Water to cover asparagus in pan
½ lemon
1 tablespoon butter, cut into small bits
3 tablespoons freshly grated Parmesan
Freshly ground black pepper

1. Preheat broiler, 15–20 minutes.

2. Break off woody part of asparagus stalks. Scrape bottoms with vegetable peeler.

3. Arrange asparagus in one layer in large pan. Add water to cover halfway up. Bring to boil over medium heat. Simmer 3 minutes.

4. Remove from heat and pour off water. Squeeze lemon over asparagus. Sprinkle with butter and cheese. Broil until cheese is completely melted. Add pepper to taste. Serve immediately.

Makes 4 portions

❧ Tomatoes with Fresh Basil

This simple dish is as delicious as it is seasonal. At the height of the tomato season, mid-August, it makes a wonderful first course. It is very important to serve the tomatoes at room temperature, when their flavor is the fullest. I had a running debate with Mayor Koch, who prefers them cold.

If your guests don't like this dish, don't invite them again.

3   medium ripe tomatoes
2   tablespoons extra virgin olive oil
½   lemon
Freshly ground black pepper
Pinch of salt
1   cup fresh basil leaves, cut into shreds

1.   Slice tomatoes ⅛ inch thick. Place on serving dish.
2.   Drizzle olive oil over tomatoes. Squeeze ½ lemon over them. Grind pepper to taste over tomatoes and sprinkle with pinch salt. Garnish with shredded basil.

Makes 4 portions

❧❧ Bruschetta alla Romana

This is my version of a dish I first tasted at Il Mulino, a restaurant in New York's Greenwich Village that serves great Italian food. The Mayor and his friends dine there often, as do I.

This very simple, very delicious appetizer takes minutes to prepare, and all you need are good ripe tomatoes and fresh basil.

3   medium ripe tomatoes (*or* 6 plum tomatoes)
3   cloves garlic, peeled and crushed
Salt and freshly ground black pepper
6   leaves fresh basil
4   tablespoons fragrant olive oil
4   slices French or Italian bread, toasted

1.   Cut tomatoes into medium dice. Place in bowl. Add garlic, salt and pepper to taste, basil, and oil. Mix well.
2.   Chill slightly and serve on bread slices.

Makes 4 portions

⚜ Roasted Vegetables

This appetizer may seem modest in its preparation, but it was high on the list of Ed Koch's "best" recipes—a list totaling about three hundred.

2   medium tomatoes
2   medium red onions
4   fresh carrots
2   medium parsnips
2   medium zucchini
½   pound shiitake mushrooms
2   tablespoons olive oil
Freshly ground black pepper
½   tablespoon dried thyme

1.   Preheat oven to 425°F.

2.   Prepare vegetables: Cut tomatoes in half. Peel onions. Scrub carrots and remove green tops but do not scrape. Scrub parsnips but do not scrape. Cut zucchini lengthwise into halves. Remove stems from mushrooms (reserve for another use).

3.   Arrange all vegetables in a flat pan or a roasting pan in one layer. Brush with olive oil and sprinkle with black pepper and thyme to taste. Roast 15 minutes or until lightly browned; turn, brush with olive oil, and roast another 15 minutes.

Makes 4 portions

❧ Broiled Wild Mushrooms

I have never been able to figure out if the Mayor liked this dish more for the garlic or the mushrooms, but I like it because it takes only 5 minutes to prepare.

1 pound shiitake mushrooms
Freshly ground black pepper
2 tablespoons olive oil
4 cloves garlic, peeled and mashed
2 tablespoons chopped parsley

1. Preheat broiler.
2. Remove stems from mushrooms. Place mushroom caps on a flat pan in one layer. Grind black pepper over them and drizzle with 1 tablespoon of the olive oil.
3. Broil 2 minutes; remove pan from broiler. Turn over mushrooms and drizzle with remaining olive oil. Broil 2 minutes. (Shake pan often so mushrooms don't stick.)
4. Remove pan from broiler. Sprinkle with garlic and toss mushrooms and garlic together.
5. Return pan to broiler and broil 30 seconds more. Remove from broiler, sprinkle mushrooms with parsley, and serve immediately.

Makes 4 portions

❧❧❧ Marinated Zucchini

This cookbook would be incomplete if I omitted this delicious vegetable snack, one of Mayor Koch's favorites. It is spicy, garlicky, and, unfortunately, fattening, since the zucchini must be deep fried.

6   small zucchini
½   cup flour
Oil for frying zucchini
2   red chili peppers
2   cloves garlic, peeled and mashed
½   medium red onion, cut into small dice
Salt
3   tablespoons olive oil

1. Slice zucchini into very thin rounds. Sprinkle with flour and shake off excess.

2. Pour oil into a frying pan to a depth of 2 inches and heat until very hot but do not burn. Fry zucchini in oil until golden brown.

3. Carefully halve and seed chili peppers. (Take care not to touch your eyes because chili pepper oil is extremely irritating.) Chop peppers together with garlic and onion until fine. Place garlic, onion, and pepper mixture in a bowl.

4. As zucchini browns, remove it to top of garlic-pepper-onion mixture. The hot oil clinging to the zucchini will wilt the onions. When all the zucchini has been removed, mix the vegetables well. Add a little salt to taste and drizzle with 3 tablespoons olive oil.

5. Marinate in the refrigerator 2–3 hours. Serve cold or at room temperature.

Makes 4 portions

❧❧❧ Grilled Marinated Tomatoes with Basil

This appetizer presents the perfect flavor combination: ripe tomatoes, basil, garlic, and balsamic vinegar.

Olive oil for greasing baking sheet and brushing tomatoes
¼ cup olive oil
¼ cup balsamic vinegar
1 clove garlic, peeled and mashed
2 large ripe tomatoes
Freshly ground black pepper
4 slices fresh mozzarella cheese, ⅛ inch thick
4 large basil leaves

1. Prepare barbecue grill or preheat broiler. Lightly grease a baking sheet with olive oil.

2. Prepare marinade: combine ¼ cup olive oil, vinegar, and garlic.

3. Slice tomatoes in half and arrange on baking sheet. Grind black pepper to taste over tomatoes. Brush with olive oil.

4. Place tomatoes on grill, or place baking sheet with tomatoes in broiler, for 1–2 minutes. Turn tomatoes and repeat on second side.

5. Remove tomatoes from heat and place in flat dish. Cover with marinade. Marinate 3–4 hours at room temperature.

6. Place a slice of mozzarella on each serving plate. Place a tomato half on the cheese. Cover each tomato half with 1 tablespoon marinade and 1 basil leaf. Serve at room temperature or slightly chilled.

Makes 4 portions

❧ Grilled Eggplant and Tomatoes with Yogurt Sauce

I'm sorry to say Mayor Koch is not a big fan of eggplant. I served this dish anyway, because guests raved about it, and I always hoped he would come to appreciate it.

1 medium eggplant, about 1½ pounds
Olive oil to brush vegetables
2 medium tomatoes
½ cup plain low-fat or nonfat yogurt
2 cloves garlic, peeled and chopped
2 tablespoons chopped parsley

1. Preheat broiler.
2. Cut eggplant into ½-inch slices. Arrange in one layer on pan and brush with olive oil. Broil until brown. Turn over slices and repeat on second side. Since eggplant absorbs oil quickly, brush sparingly. Remove to platter.
3. Cut tomatoes into ½-inch slices and repeat process.
4. Alternate slices of eggplant and tomato on platter.
5. Mix yogurt with garlic and parsley. Spoon over sliced vegetables.

Makes 4 portions

⚜ Eggplant with Tomatoes

2 tablespoons olive oil
1 medium eggplant, unpeeled and cut into ½-inch cubes
3 cloves garlic, peeled and chopped
½ pint red cherry tomatoes, cut in halves
½ pint yellow cherry tomatoes, cut in halves
2 tablespoons chopped parsley
Salt and freshly ground black pepper

1. Heat oil in a heavy frying pan. Add eggplant and toss until cooked, 5–7 minutes.

2. Remove pan from heat. Add garlic, tomatoes, and parsley. Toss. Season with salt and pepper to taste.

Makes 4 portions

⚜ Grilled Salmon Chunks

This was a favorite hors d'oeuvre at Gracie Mansion dinner parties.

Cut the salmon into chunks large enough so that they will not fall through the grill. If you prefer to skewer the fish, you may do so, although it is not necessary.

½ cup light soy sauce
3 tablespoons sweet sake
1 tablespoon ground fresh gingerroot
1 pound salmon, skin and bones removed, cut into chunks

1. Preheat broiler or prepare a charcoal fire on a grill and let it burn down to embers.

2. Combine first three ingredients. Marinate salmon in the mixture 20 minutes.

3. Grill or broil salmon 2–3 minutes.

Makes 6–8 portions

❧ Steamed Artichokes with Yogurt and Basil Sauce

When the artichokes are fully cooked, you can remove the choke with a spoon. Chokeless, the vegetables make a more interesting presentation for your guests. The yogurt sauce is delicious on the tomato as well as on the artichokes.

4   large artichokes
4   quarts water
1   teaspoon salt
2   large tomatoes, sliced
1   cup Yogurt and Basil Sauce (see Index)

1.   Remove the outer leaves of the artichokes; trim the stems so that they can stand flat.

2.   Bring water to boil in a large pot. Add salt and artichokes. Boil about 30 minutes or until the leaves can be removed easily and the bottom is tender.

3.   Remove from pot and drain upside down.

4.   Scoop out the choke of each artichoke with a spoon.

5.   Place each artichoke on an individual plate and surround with tomato slices. Serve with Yogurt and Basil Sauce.

Makes 4 portions

⚜⚜⚜ Grilled Pizza

This recipe may seem unusual, but I made it about twice a month at Gracie Mansion, and I can guarantee it to be a 100 percent success. Grilling the pizza crust adds a unique charcoal flavor.

Use any basic pizza dough, fresh or frozen.

 2 large tomatoes, each cut into 4 thick slices
 1 tablespoon plus 4 teaspoons olive oil
Salt and freshly ground black pepper
 ½ pound pizza dough, enough for 4 6-inch pizzas
 2 Roasted Peppers (see Index), julienned
4-5 cloves garlic, peeled and crushed
 4 anchovy fillets
 ½ pound goat cheese, crumbled
 ½ pound mozzarella, grated
 1 teaspoon each fresh rosemary, oregano, and thyme (*or* ¼ teaspoon dried)

1. Prepare a wood or charcoal fire and let it burn down to embers.

2. Preheat oven to 450°F.

3. Place tomato slices on grill, brush with olive oil, and season with salt and pepper to taste. Grill 1 minute. Turn slices, brush with oil, and grill 1 more minute. Remove from grill.

4. Roll out four individual pizza shells, each 6 inches in diameter.

5. Place on grill until slightly charred. Turn and char other side. Remove from grill.

6. Place pizza shells on a cookie sheet. Divide among each, for topping, the tomatoes, peppers, garlic, anchovies, and cheeses. Sprinkle each with 1 teaspoon olive oil. Sprinkle each with a pinch of rosemary, oregano, and thyme.

7. Place in oven and bake 15–20 minutes. Serve at once.

Makes 4 portions

Variation: After removing pizzas from oven, place 1 teaspoon Pesto (see Index) on each.

Soups

Mayor Koch's Favorite Pureed Mussel Soup

Mussel Soup with Saffron

Manhattan Clam Chowder

Mushroom Soup

Dinner-in-Itself Fish Soup

Minestrone

Pureed Vegetable Soup

Gazpacho

When I talk about soups served at Gracie Mansion, I mean hearty preparations. I didn't generally serve broths, which remind me of dishwater. No matter how long the cook slaves over the perfect consommé, he still has a bowl of clear liquid to serve his guests. It seems to me that they are usually not too impressed. (Chicken broth, which has its own mystique, is an exception to this rule, as I mention below.)

But real soups are a different matter. They are inexpensive, healthful, filling, beautiful, and delicious. Made the lightened way, they contain no butter, cream, or flour. They are perfect as a dinner course or as a complete lunch.

A good soup is simplicity itself to prepare, once the stock upon which it is based is made. As I say in the section on stocks, all you need for many meals can be made in one day and frozen. Defrost a container of fish stock when you want to cook a clam chowder or a container of chicken stock when you have a cold. (Whenever someone got sick at Gracie Mansion, out came the chicken broth. The Mayor has taken chicken soup to such friends as Cardinal O'Connor and former Manhattan Borough President Percy Sutton when they were ailing.)

Mayor Koch enjoyed the soups I served him. Some of his favorites were puree of mussel, fish soup, and puree of winter vegetables. The mussel puree typifies a formerly rich recipe that I lightened and improved. It is made with steamed mussels and requires no butter, flour, or cream. The vegetable puree is a fantastic recipe. Based on chicken stock, it needs no cream or other enrichment. The fish soup, Provençale in origin, is a perfect meal alone, with a light pasta, or with a salad. It contains a variety of fresh fish, shellfish, vegetables, and herbs, which are simmered together and then pureed. I must admit it is complicated and time-consuming to prepare, so plan to make it only when you have enough time. You will be happy you did—it is fantastic.

For myself, I feel you can't beat a cup of steaming Minestrone or vegetable-rich Manhattan Clam Chowder on a winter evening. On a warm summer night, a cold, garlic-rich Gazpacho made with ripe tomatoes is positively heavenly.

When I first came to Gracie Mansion, I made a rich, thick cream of mushroom soup. As I have done with so many dishes, I subsequently lightened and improved it. I cut way back on flour and totally cut out butter and cream. It is now on the thin side, and so are the people who enjoy it.

⚜ Mayor Koch's Favorite Pureed Mussel Soup

This soup quickly became one of the Mayor's most frequent requests. It has absolutely no salt, butter, oil, or cream, and he loved it anyway.

4 quarts mussels, well scrubbed
1 onion, minced
6 shallots, peeled and mashed
4 sprigs parsley
2 cups dry white wine
2 quarts Fish Stock (see Index)
Freshly ground black pepper

1. Put cleaned mussels in a large pot with onion, shallots, parsley, and wine. Bring to a boil and simmer until mussels open.

2. Remove mussels from pot and discard any that have not opened. Remove opened mussels from shells and discard shells.

3. Put vegetables and half the mussels in food processor, reserving half the mussels for garnish, and blend until smooth.

4. Add Fish Stock to poaching liquid and bring to a simmer. Add pureed mussel mixture and pepper to taste. Serve very hot, garnished with reserved mussels.

Makes about 2 quarts

❧❧❧ Mussel Soup with Saffron

I wrestled with my conscience about including this recipe. In no way is it light, since it contains 1 cup cream for six to eight diners. You can't avoid the cream—so either skip the soup altogether or be very careful with the rest of your meal.

2   tablespoons olive oil
1   fennel bulb, sliced
6   sprigs parsley
½   onion, peeled and sliced
2   carrots, scraped and sliced
2   cups dry white wine
4   dozen mussels in shells, cleaned well
Bones from 4–5 flounder or sole (optional)
Water to cover
Salt and freshly ground black pepper
1   small (.2 gram) package saffron
1   cup heavy cream

1.   Heat oil in a large soup pot. Add fennel, parsley, onion, and carrots. Cook slowly 10 minutes, taking care not to brown.

2.   Add wine and cook 3 minutes. Add mussels and fish bones, if desired. Add water to cover. Simmer 20 minutes.

3.   Strain through fine sieve to remove mussels and bones, reserving broth. Discard fish bones. Remove mussels from shells, discarding any that have not opened. Simmer broth 20 minutes more. Season with salt and pepper to taste. Remove ½ cup soup from pot and mix in saffron. Just before serving, add cream, mussels, and the saffron mixture to remaining soup.

Makes 1½–2 quarts

❧ Manhattan Clam Chowder

All the vegetables that go into this soup should be cut by hand into medium dice. Don't use a food processor! One of our recipe testers processed the vegetables and produced a mystery soup—absolutely delicious, but not clam chowder.

24 chowder clams, well scrubbed
Water to cover clams, about 2 quarts
 3 tablespoons olive oil
 3 large Spanish onions, peeled and chopped coarse
 4 ribs celery, chopped coarse
 3 red peppers, seeded and chopped coarse
 1 green pepper, seeded and chopped coarse
 5 Idaho potatoes, about 2½ pounds, peeled and quartered
 6 cloves garlic, peeled and mashed
 6 cups canned whole tomatoes, drained and crushed
Dash Tabasco sauce (optional)

1. Place clams in a large 2-gallon saucepan (or 2 smaller pots if necessary) and cover with water; bring to boil. When clams open, remove from shells and discard shells. Discard any unopened clams. Remove stock and retain. There should be about 2 quarts.

2. In same saucepan, heat olive oil and sauté onions until transparent. Add celery and peppers and cook 2–3 minutes over medium heat.

3. Add potatoes, garlic, and tomatoes. Cook 1 minute.

4. Add reserved clam stock. Simmer 1½ hours, until reduced. Stock should simmer steadily but should not boil.

5. About 30 minutes before serving, chop clams (this can be done in a processor). Add to hot soup immediately before serving. Add Tabasco sauce, if desired.

Makes about 2 quarts

❧ Mushroom Soup

I served this fragrant soup at all Mayor Koch's Gracie Mansion Thanksgiving dinners.

2 teaspoons light olive oil
½ cup chopped shallots
4 pounds mushrooms, chopped fine
4 tablespoons flour
2 quarts Chicken Stock (see Index)
Salt and freshly ground black pepper
¼ cup fresh thyme

1. Heat oil in a large pan. Add shallots and cook until lightly browned.

2. Add mushrooms and cook over medium heat until mushrooms are dry. (This will take 8–10 minutes because of their high water content.)

3. Turn heat to low. Add flour and cook 10 minutes.

4. Raise heat to medium. Add 2 cups Chicken Stock, stirring until liquid thickens. Add remainder of stock.

5. Simmer until soup is reduced by one-third. Add salt and pepper to taste and thyme.

Makes 2 quarts

❧ Dinner-in-Itself Fish Soup

This is not a soup, it is an experience. It is my version of the Mediterranean fish soup so popular in the south of France. Consistency and texture determine the excellence of this soup, and they, in turn, depend upon your ingredients. The more fish and seafood you use, the better your soup becomes. As you can see, my recipe calls for generous quantities of lobsters, clams, mussels, and sea bass.

This recipe is expensive and time-consuming. Try it anyway for your next important party. The flavor is worth the time, and the yield is worth the expense.

3   tablespoons olive oil
3   medium Spanish onions, peeled and sliced
3   live lobsters, each about 1½ pounds, sliced in half down the back and then cut into halves again (have this done at the fish market)
3   pounds sea bass, cleaned and chopped into quarters, including head and tail (have this done at the fish market)
6   cloves garlic, peeled and mashed
6   medium tomatoes, chopped roughly into large dice
2   cups white wine
1   dozen littleneck clams, rinsed well under cold water
2   dozen mussels, scrubbed
4   quarts Fish Stock (see Index), or enough to cover all the ingredients; if necessary, add up to 2 quarts water (stock will reduce in cooking)
5   sprigs fresh thyme
4   sprigs parsley
1   tablespoon tomato paste
Salt and freshly ground black pepper
1   tablespoon grated Gruyère cheese per serving

1.   Heat olive oil in a large pot. Add onions and brown slightly. Add lobsters and fish and mix well. Add garlic and tomatoes. Mix thoroughly and cook 2 minutes.

2.   Add wine. Cook 2 minutes to reduce. Add clams, mussels, and stock and bring to boil.

3.   Simmer 10–15 minutes, skimming any foam that rises to the top.

4.   Add thyme and parsley. Simmer 1 hour.

5.   With a large spoon, remove fish and shellfish and set aside to cool. Let soup continue to cook slowly.

6. Once fish and shellfish have cooled, carefully remove all meat. Discard shells, skin, and bones.

7. Puree the meat in a food processor with a little of the soup. Do this in batches if necessary. Return the puree to the pot of soup. Add the tomato paste and stir well. The soup should be orange-red in color and thick in consistency. Add salt and pepper to taste.

8. Sprinkle each serving with 1 tablespoon grated Gruyère cheese.

Makes 5-6 quarts

❧ Minestrone

As with any soup, the longer you simmer it, the thicker and tastier it becomes.

3 tablespoons olive oil
2 stalks celery, diced
2 medium onions, peeled and diced
4 white turnips, scraped and diced
3 medium Idaho potatoes, with skin, diced
2 red peppers, seeded and diced
2 cloves garlic, peeled and crushed
1 tomato, seeded and chopped
Salt and freshly ground black pepper
6 cups Brown Veal Stock (see Index)
1 Bouquet Garni (see Index)
2 cups red kidney beans, cooked or canned, and drained

1. Heat oil in a heavy soup pot. Add vegetables all at once. Add garlic. Sauté for 10 minutes without browning. Add tomato and mix well. Sprinkle with salt and pepper to taste.

2. Add stock and bring to a simmer. Add Bouquet Garni and beans. (You can mash or puree beans if you like; this will help to thicken soup.) Simmer for 2 hours, stirring often. Take care that soup does not burn as it thickens. Remove Bouquet Garni before serving.

Makes 1½ quarts

❧ Pureed Vegetable Soup

This soup is thickened by pureeing and reduction—no thickening ingredients are added to the fresh vegetables and stock. Its beautiful amber color is the result of keeping it at a gentle simmer.

3   medium Spanish onions, peeled
1   bunch carrots, scraped
3   white radishes, scraped
5   medium turnips, scraped
2   heads broccoli, cleaned
2   heads cauliflower
1   bunch flat-leaf (Italian) parsley
2   cloves garlic, peeled
3   tablespoons olive oil
3   quarts Chicken Stock (see Index)
2   bay leaves
Salt and freshly ground black pepper
6   sprigs fresh thyme (*or* ¼ teaspoon dried)

    1.   Rough cut all vegetables into medium dice.

    2.   Heat oil in a heavy soup pot and add onions and carrots. Cook slowly 15 minutes. Add remaining vegetables and garlic and cook over low heat until all vegetables are soft.

    3.   Add stock and bring to a gentle boil. Add bay leaf. Simmer for 30 minutes. As the soup cooks and reduces, it will thicken slightly.

    4.   Remove vegetables and place in a food processor fitted with a metal blade. Process to a rough puree. (Some texture enhances the soup.)

    5.   Return to pot and simmer until it has reduced to desired thickness. Season with salt, pepper, and thyme to taste.

Makes 3 quarts

⚜⚜ Gazpacho

This cold soup was a summer favorite at Gracie Mansion. To suit Mayor Koch's taste, I sometimes increased the amount of garlic.

8   large ripe tomatoes
3   red peppers, seeded
2   red Spanish onions, peeled
4   large shallots, peeled
3   cucumbers
4   cloves garlic, peeled
¾   cup red wine vinegar
½   cup olive oil
1½ cups tomato juice
Salt and freshly ground black pepper
Dash Tabasco sauce
½   cup chopped fresh dill

1.   Coarsely chop tomatoes and peppers. Slice onions and shallots. Peel, seed, and coarsely chop cucumbers.

2.   Place vegetables and garlic in a food processor fitted with the metal blade. Blend to a chunky consistency.

3.   Combine vinegar, oil, and tomato juice. Add processed vegetables to vinegar mixture. Add salt and pepper to taste, Tabasco, and dill.

Makes 2 quarts

Pasta

Angel Hair Pasta with Olive Oil and Basil

Angel Hair Pasta with Tomatoes, Garlic, and Basil

Fettuccine with Chanterelles

Fettuccine with Tomato Sauce and Steamed Vegetables

Fettuccine with Goat Cheese, Basil, and Red Peppers

Angel Hair Pasta with Sun-Dried Tomatoes

Fettuccine Primavera with Ricotta Cheese

Angel Hair Pasta with Roasted Peppers

Pasta with Shiitake Mushrooms

Papardelle with Leeks and Sun-Dried Tomatoes

Fettuccine with Porcini

Fusilli with Zucchini, Prosciutto, and Romano

Once upon a time, before the New York City Marathon, pasta was considered fattening. Now we know that it is fattening only if it is bathed in rich sauces and smothered in cheese. Depending upon your discretion in accompaniments, you can eat pasta and still keep slim and healthy.

Pasta is wonderfully adaptable. You can use countless different sauces on the same noodle. Mayor Koch would willingly eat pasta five nights a week. For him, of course, garlic is the ultimate accompaniment, and I find it goes well with many different sauces.

Pasta spans the seasons. It is a great winter first course, and in the summer, preceded by a salad of fresh tomatoes and basil, it is my favorite light meal.

Fresh pasta is quite chic, and when I was young and naive, I often made my own. However, experience has taught me that dried pasta is preferable to fresh: it is more robust, it stands up to sauces, it is easily stored. Ease of preparation and convenience are cornerstones of my recipes, and cranking out fresh pasta is not my idea of either.

In the Gracie Mansion kitchen I relied on angel hair and fettuccine for many dishes. Angel hair works well with the lighter sauces, such as those made with sun-dried tomatoes and fresh herbs. Fettuccine's texture lends itself to more robust sauces, such as those using porcini and vegetables.

Nothing could be easier than preparing pasta. For four people, you need a large pot that can hold at least 4 quarts of water. Bring this water to a rolling boil and then add 2 tablespoons of oil and 2 teaspoons of salt. Add the pasta in several batches, so that the water temperature does not go down quickly. Bring the water back to a furious boil, stir, and cook pasta until done to your taste (my taste is for slightly underdone, or al dente, which takes a couple of minutes less than the time recommended on the box).

If you want a lighter meal, you may prepare the pasta without any oil or salt in the water.

♣♣ Angel Hair Pasta with Olive Oil and Basil

This is the simplest pasta recipe imaginable, and it can be prepared in 10 minutes. If you rely on your common sense in putting everything together, it is a model of efficiency. First put up the water to boil. While it is heating, wash, dry, and julienne the basil. Once the pasta is cooking, you have just enough time to grate the cheese. Through all this, warm your serving bowl in a slow oven. Drain the cooked pasta, combine the other ingredients, and your pasta course is complete, fresh, and perfect. It must be served at once.

4   quarts water
2   teaspoons salt
4   tablespoons olive oil
1   pound angel hair pasta
Freshly ground black pepper
2   cups fresh basil leaves, julienned
½   cup grated Parmesan

    1.   Warm serving bowl in oven. Heat water in a large pot. When it comes to a boil, add salt and 2 tablespoons of the oil. Add pasta and cook to taste. Drain pasta and place in a heated bowl.

    2.   Drizzle remaining oil over pasta. Season generously with pepper. Toss with basil and cheese.

Makes 4 portions

❧ Angel Hair Pasta with Tomatoes, Garlic, and Basil

This was one of my favorite pasta dishes because all of its ingredients were usually on hand at Gracie Mansion. It was easy to get this on the table in 15 minutes, start to finish.

 4   quarts water
 3   tablespoons olive oil
10   plum tomatoes, chopped into medium dice
 2   cloves garlic, peeled and mashed
Freshly ground black pepper
 2   teaspoons salt
 1   pound angel hair pasta
 2   cups fresh basil leaves, washed, dried, and julienned
 4   tablespoons grated Parmesan

1. Bring water to a boil in a large pot.
2. Meanwhile, heat 1 tablespoon of the oil in a large frying pan. Add tomatoes and toss twice. Add garlic and pepper to taste and cook 3 minutes. Set aside.
3. When water boils, add salt and the remaining 2 tablespoons oil. Add pasta and cook to taste. Drain pasta.
4. As you remove pasta from heat, return tomatoes to medium heat.
5. Add pasta to tomato sauce. Mix well.
6. Add julienned basil leaves to pasta. Add cheese. Serve immediately.

Makes 4 portions

❧ Fettuccine with Chanterelles

Chanterelles have a very delicate flavor, so go easy on the grated Parmesan. But a lot of pepper is nice.

3   tablespoons light olive oil
1¼ pounds chanterelles, cleaned and trimmed of stems
4   quarts water
2   teaspoons salt
1   pound fettuccine
4   sprigs fresh basil
Freshly ground black pepper
2   tablespoons grated Parmesan

   1.   Heat 1 tablespoon of the oil in a large pan. Add chanterelles and toss over high heat, 2 minutes.

   2.   Heat water in a large pot. When it comes to a boil, add salt and remaining 2 tablespoons oil. Add fettuccine and cook to taste.

   3.   Drain fettuccine. Add to pan with chanterelles and toss well. Add basil, pepper, and Parmesan and toss again. Serve immediately—this must be served hot.

Makes 4 portions

Fettuccine with Tomato Sauce and Steamed Vegetables

This dish exemplifies what we have tried to accomplish by lightening the cuisine of Gracie Mansion. Although it is low in calories, it is interesting and beautiful, as well as tasty. The tomato sauce should be well seasoned, because the flavor of the finished dish depends upon it. Toss the vegetables with fresh herbs and freshly ground black pepper.

½   pound snow peas
1   head broccoli
1   pound medium asparagus
½   cup water for steaming vegetables
4   cups Light Tomato Sauce (see Index)
4   quarts water
2   teaspoons salt
2   tablespoons olive oil
1   pound fettuccine
½   cup grated Parmesan
Freshly ground black pepper

1.   Wash vegetables and prepare as follows: Cut snow peas in half on an angle. Break off broccoli flowers (discard stems or reserve for another use). Break off asparagus tips (discard stalks or reserve for another use).

2.   Place ½ cup water in bottom of a large pot. Bring to a boil and add vegetables. Steam 2 minutes. (Alternatively, you can place them in a steamer basket above boiling water.)

3.   Heat Light Tomato Sauce to simmer. In a food processor, process the tomato sauce for about 10 seconds. Keep sauce hot.

4.   Bring 4 quarts water to a boil in a large pot. Add salt and oil. Add pasta and cook to taste. Drain pasta and return to cooking pot. Add vegetables, sauce, and cheese. Season with pepper.

Makes 4 portions

❧❧❧ Fettuccine with Goat Cheese, Basil, and Red Peppers

Red peppers give this pasta dish a beautiful color. They also go wonderfully with the goat cheese. However, the cheese takes this dish into the rich category.

4 quarts water
1 teaspoon salt
3 tablespoons olive oil
1 pound fettuccine
4 Roasted Peppers, julienned (see Index)
1 cup goat cheese, such as Montrachet or Boucheron
2 bunches fresh basil, leaves only
Salt and freshly ground black pepper

1. Heat water in a large pot. When it comes to a boil, add salt and 2 tablespoons oil. Add fettuccine and cook to taste. Drain.

2. While pasta is cooking, heat remaining olive oil in a large frying pan and sauté red peppers. Add cooked pasta to pan. Add goat cheese, half of the basil, and salt and black pepper to taste. Toss quickly and serve immediately, garnished with the remaining basil.

Makes 4 portions

❧ Angel Hair Pasta with Sun-Dried Tomatoes

This light pasta dish was perfectly suited to Mayor Koch. First, he loves garlic. Second, he loves sun-dried tomatoes. Third, he loves pasta. And most important, the entire recipe took me 10 minutes to prepare.

4   quarts water
5   tablespoons olive oil
2   teaspoons salt
1   pound angel hair pasta
2   cloves garlic, peeled and mashed
8   sun-dried tomatoes, cut into thin strips
¼   cup freshly grated Parmesan

1.   Heat water in a large pot. When it comes to a boil, add 2 tablespoons of the oil and salt. Add pasta and cook to taste; drain.

2.   In a large pan, heat remaining 3 tablespoons olive oil. Add garlic and cook 1 minute. Add tomatoes and pasta and mix well over medium heat. Add cheese and serve immediately.

Makes 4 portions

❧❧❧ Fettuccine Primavera with Ricotta Cheese

I have omitted the cream sauce that is traditional to this recipe, and I found that almost no one missed it. The cheese still keeps this out of the light category, but it is very much lighter than the original version.

5 tablespoons olive oil
1 dozen medium asparagus tips
2 medium zucchini, cut into ¼-inch rounds
2 cups sliced mushrooms
2 cloves garlic, peeled and crushed
½ pound snow peas, sliced on the diagonal into ½-inch pieces
3 medium tomatoes (about 2 pounds), cut into large dice
Salt and freshly ground black pepper
4 quarts water
1 teaspoon salt
1 pound fettuccine
1½ cups part skim-milk ricotta cheese

1. Heat 3 tablespoons of the olive oil in large pan. Add asparagus tips and stir until tips turn bright green. Add zucchini, mushrooms, garlic, and snow peas and sauté 2 minutes. Add tomatoes and stir. Add salt and pepper to taste.

2. Meanwhile, bring water to boil in a large pot. Add salt and the remaining 2 tablespoons of oil and cook fettuccine until done to taste. Drain.

3. Add fettuccine to pan with vegetables. Toss quickly over low heat.

4. Add ricotta cheese and serve immediately.

Makes 4 portions

❧❧❧ Angel Hair Pasta with Roasted Peppers

This dish is perfect in more than one way. It is delicious, easy to prepare, and garnished with fresh basil, it makes a wonderful presentation.

3   Roasted Peppers (see Index)
2   cloves garlic, peeled and crushed
4   tablespoons olive oil, separated
Salt and freshly ground black pepper
4   quarts water
2   teaspoons salt
1   pound angel hair pasta
1   cup fresh basil, julienned
½   pound thinly sliced prosciutto, julienned
4   tablespoons grated Parmesan (optional)

1.   Cut roasted peppers into julienne.

2.   Combine garlic, 2 tablespoons of the oil, and salt and pepper to taste. Toss peppers with mixture.

3.   Heat water in a large pot. When it comes to a boil, add 2 teaspoons salt and the remaining 2 tablespoons oil. Add pasta and cook briefly. It will be done when water returns to the boil.

4.   In a large pan, heat peppers. Drain pasta and add to pan. Add basil and prosciutto. Mix thoroughly and serve at once. Sprinkle each serving with 1 tablespoon Parmesan if desired.

Makes 4 portions

❧ Pasta with Shiitake Mushrooms

Make this dish with the pasta of your choice. The shiitake mushrooms complement both the delicate and the more robust types of pasta.

4   tablespoons olive oil
¾   pound shiitake mushrooms, cleaned and sliced
4   quarts water
2   teaspoons salt
1   pound pasta
Freshly ground black pepper

    1.   Heat 2 tablespoons of the olive oil and sauté mushrooms over high heat until slightly crisp.

    2.   Heat water in a large pot; when it comes to a boil, add salt and the remaining 2 tablespoons olive oil. Add pasta and cook to taste.

    3.   Drain pasta and immediately add hot mushrooms. Grind pepper over all. Serve immediately.

Makes 4 portions

Variation: Add 1 cup heavy cream to sautéed mushrooms and cook until reduced by half. Add to drained pasta as above. Note that the addition of cream changes the rating from light to rich.

❧❧❧ Papardelle with Leeks and Sun-Dried Tomatoes

I have included this recipe simply because it is too delicious to leave out. It calls for a small amount of heavy cream—1 cup to serve four people. Nevertheless, this qualifies it as rich, and it should be served as part of a balanced menu.

Papardelle are square noodles, which are prepared in exactly the same way as other pastas. They aren't served by home cooks very much—you usually see them in restaurants. They are delicious, and their shape makes them easy to eat.

4   quarts water
2   teaspoons salt
3   tablespoons olive oil
1   pound papardelle
1   leek, washed well to remove all sand
2   sun-dried tomatoes
1   cup heavy cream

1.   Heat water in a large pot. When it comes to a boil, add salt and 2 tablespoons of the oil. Add papardelle and cook to taste. Drain.

2.   Use only the white part of the leek. Cut into julienne.

3.   Cut sun-dried tomatoes into julienne.

4.   Heat remaining 1 tablespoon olive oil in medium pan. Sauté leek strips. When slightly browned, add julienned tomatoes. Toss over medium heat.

5.   Raise heat and add heavy cream; heat thoroughly, but do not allow cream to reduce.

6.   Add pasta to sauce. Mix and serve at once.

Makes 4 portions

⚜⚜ Fettuccine with Porcini

Porcini are fantastic tasting as well as quite expensive. Use wisely.

1   pound porcini, stems as well as caps, cleaned and
        trimmed as needed
1   tablespoon butter
3   tablespoons olive oil
4   quarts water
2   teaspoons salt
1   pound fettuccine
4   tablespoons grated Parmesan
Freshly ground black pepper
¼   cup fresh herb mixture: basil, thyme, tarragon, and chervil,
        minced (optional)

1.   Cut porcini into halves or quarters.

2.   Heat butter and 1 tablespoon of the olive oil in a large pan. Brown porcini slightly over high heat.

3.   Heat water in a large pot. When it comes to a boil, add salt and remaining 2 tablespoons olive oil. Add fettuccine and cook to taste.

4.   Drain pasta. Add to mushrooms in pan. Toss, sprinkle with Parmesan and pepper to taste. Add optional herbs and serve immediately.

Makes 4 portions

❧❧❧ Fusilli with Zucchini, Prosciutto, and Romano

This is a great recipe for the corkscrew pasta known as fusilli, and I include it despite its sinful mixture of cream, prosciutto, and cheese. It doesn't require any additional salt because of the cheese and prosciutto. Cut the zucchini into cubes to prevent its overcooking and to keep it crisp.

4   quarts water
1   teaspoon salt
3   tablespoons olive oil
1   pound fusilli
2   small, firm zucchini
1   cup heavy cream
4   tablespoons grated Romano
¼   pound prosciutto, cut into strips
½   cup shredded basil leaves
Freshly ground black pepper

1.   Heat water in a large pot. When it comes to a boil, add salt and 2 tablespoons of the oil. Add pasta and cook to taste.

2.   While pasta is cooking, wash zucchini and cut into medium cubes.

3.   Heat 1 tablespoon oil in a frying pan and sauté zucchini 1 minute. Remove from heat. Drain cooked pasta and place in pan with zucchini. Toss over high heat; add cream and cook 2 minutes. Add cheese and toss well. Remove from heat. Add prosciutto and toss again. Add basil, season with pepper to taste, and serve at once.

Makes 4 portions

Fish

Broiled Shad

Broiled Whole Baby Flounder

Poached Halibut on a Bed of Grilled Leeks

Red Snapper with Saffron

Roasted Salmon

Poached Salmon with Dill and Yogurt Sauce

Poached Salmon with Sorrel Sauce

Salmon Steaks with Black Beans

Salmon en Papillote

Sautéed Scallops of Salmon

Grilled Sardines

Grilled Marinated Scallops of Salmon

Grilled Sole

Steamed Fillet of Sole with Duxelles, Wrapped in Spinach

Roasted Striped Bass

Roasted Striped Bass with Roasted Fennel

Swordfish en Brochette

Trout with Lemon and Butter

Grilled Marinated Tuna

I served fish abundantly at Gracie Mansion. First of all, fish is low in fat and calories. And aside from its obvious healthful qualities, it is among the quickest foods to prepare. It seemed to fit well into our schedule: if Mayor Koch arrived home at 9:35, his main course of fish could be served at 9:45.

Fish is always elegant and special, because it is cooked to order. That quality of freshness cannot be matched. Fillets and steaks can be broiled, grilled, poached, sautéed, or steamed. Whole fish (which of course takes longest to prepare) can also be roasted or baked.

Fine fish is available all year round, but you should find a reliable fishmonger. When buying whole fish, look for red gills, bright eyes, and firm flesh. If fish does not have the freshest smell, don't buy it. Fillets and steaks should be firm to the touch, never mushy.

❧❧ Broiled Shad

During shad's brief season, I served it many times to Mayor Koch, at his request. In fact, I think that I got tired of cooking it before he got tired of eating it.

Marinade
¼ cup olive oil
Juice of 1 lemon
1 bay leaf
4 sprigs parsley
½ tablespoon dried thyme

Fish
2 pounds shad fillets
4 lemon wedges for garnish

1. Preheat broiler to very hot, about 15–25 minutes.

2. Combine marinade ingredients. Add fish fillets and marinate 1 hour, turning twice.

3. Remove fish from the marinade but do not dry. Place skin-side down on broiler rack and broil 6–8 minutes. Fish should be golden brown. Serve garnished with lemon wedges.

Makes 4 portions

❧ Broiled Whole Baby Flounder

If you cannot get baby flounder, you can prepare flounder fillets according to this recipe, and they will be delicious. But the whole flounder are really extraordinary, and the bones can be removed with ease.

4   whole baby flounder, approximately ¾ pound each, cleaned
        and heads and tips of tails removed (have this done at the
        fish market)
½   teaspoon sea salt or kosher salt
Freshly ground black pepper
2   tablespoons butter, melted
Juice of 2 lemons
2   tablespoons chopped parsley

1.   Preheat broiler until very hot, 15–25 minutes.

2.   Arrange fish on baking sheet, belly (white) side up. Season lightly with salt and pepper to taste. Brush lightly with melted butter and lemon juice. Broil 3 minutes.

3.   Turn fish over and repeat process. During the last 3 minutes of broiling brush with butter and lemon juice approximately every minute.

4.   Remove from broiler and place on plates. Sprinkle with chopped parsley.

Makes 4 portions

❧ Poached Halibut on a Bed of Grilled Leeks

Although this recipe involves two separate cooking steps, grilling and poaching, it is really quite simple. In the end, the grilled vegetables and the poached fish make a wonderful combination of textures, flavors, and aromas.

3   cups Court Bouillon (see Index)
4   halibut steaks, about 6 ounces each
3   bunches small leeks, well washed
Olive oil for brushing leeks
Salt and freshly ground black pepper
2   cups Light Tomato Sauce (see Index)

    1.   Prepare a charcoal or wood fire and let it burn down to embers.

    2.   Bring Court Bouillon to a simmer and poach fish 5–6 minutes. Do not overcook. Keep fish warm in the poaching liquid.

    3.   Meanwhile, trim leeks, retaining white part and about 1 inch of stem, place on the grill, and cook about 10 minutes until they are slightly browned, turning once. Brush with a little oil to aid browning. It is important that they be thoroughly grilled.

    4.   Divide leeks among four dinner plates. Place a poached halibut steak on top of leeks. Season with salt and pepper to taste. Serve with tomato sauce on the side.

Makes 4 portions

⚜⚜ Red Snapper with Saffron

Don't be afraid of the butter in this recipe. It makes the sauce wonderfully smooth, and less than 1 tablespoon per person won't hurt. Just be sure to watch the rest of your menu! This is an elegant main course for a dinner party.

3   cups Fish Stock (see Index)
½   cup white wine
4   red snapper fillets, about 6 ounces each
Freshly ground white pepper
1   small (.2 gram) package saffron
3   tablespoons cold butter, cut into small pieces

1.   Bring stock and wine to simmer.

2.   Run the blade of a sharp knife across the skin of each fillet. This will help prevent the fillets from shrinking when cooked. Season fillets with pepper to taste.

3.   Place fish in stock and simmer until firm to the touch, 4–5 minutes. Remove and keep warm.

4.   Place saffron in a cup or small bowl with 3 tablespoons stock and put aside.

5.   Reduce remaining stock by two-thirds and add saffron mix. Remove from heat and add the cold butter pieces, stirring to incorporate them. This sauce will have a beautiful golden tint, from the saffron.

6.   Place fillets on individual plates and cover with sauce.

Makes 4 portions

❧❧ Roasted Salmon

This makes a special presentation at a summer dinner party. A whole salmon serves ten in royal style and is as good cold as it is hot. Light Tomato Sauce (see Index) complements this dish well.

1   whole salmon, 6–7 pounds, cleaned and filleted
Salt and freshly ground black pepper
4   tablespoons olive oil
2   pounds domestic mushrooms, chopped fine
1   fennel bulb, sliced into ⅛-inch pieces
5   sprigs fresh tarragon
Kitchen string for tying the fish

1.   Preheat oven to 450°F.

2.   Remove with a tweezers any small bones remaining in the salmon. Salt and pepper fish lightly.

3.   Heat 2 tablespoons of the olive oil and sauté mushrooms over high heat until all the moisture has evaporated to make Duxelles (see Index).

4.   Place one fillet of fish skin side down on a work surface. Spread fennel over fish. Mound mushrooms on top of fennel. Arrange fresh tarragon sprigs over mushrooms.

5.   Cover with the second fillet. Tie stuffed fillets securely with string.

6.   Heat remaining 2 tablespoons olive oil in an oval pan large enough to accommodate the fish. Over high heat, brown both sides of the fish until the skin is very crisp.

7.   Place fish in oven and roast for 15 to 20 minutes. Remove from oven and let rest 10 to 15 minutes before slicing. To serve, slice and place on serving plate or individual dinner plates. Spoon Light Tomato Sauce around fish, if desired.

Makes 10 portions

Variation: You can also have the fishmonger remove the bones without separating the fillets, which will make the fish more manageable.

❧ Poached Salmon with Dill and Yogurt Sauce

You can prepare this fish in a fish poacher, placing the salmon on a rack in the simmering Court Bouillon. Or you can use a large pot and wrap the fish in cheesecloth and then place it in the bouillon. Prepare your court bouillon directly in the pot or poacher you will use for the salmon. Poach the fish slowly, never letting the liquid come to a boil.

Poached Salmon
Court Bouillon to cover fish, about 8 cups (see Index)
1   whole salmon, about 6–7 pounds

Dill and Yogurt Sauce
2   tablespoons fresh dill
1   cup plain low-fat or nonfat yogurt
Pinch salt

1.   First, make Court Bouillon in a fish poacher or large pot. Bring to a simmer and cook 25 minutes.

2.   Place fish in the simmering liquid. If there is not enough bouillon to cover fish, add water. Poach fish 25 minutes.

3.   Remove fish from poacher and let rest 15 minutes. Run a sharp knife along the back of the fish and gently peel away the skin. Then slowly scrape away the gray fatty substance under the skin with a knife.

4.   Run a knife down the center of the fish to separate the two fillets. Each fillet can be cut into 5–6 portions.

5.   Prepare sauce: Mince dill by running knife through it once. Combine all ingredients.

6.   Serve salmon hot or at room temperature accompanied by the Dill and Yogurt Sauce.

Makes 10–12 portions

❦❦ Poached Salmon with Sorrel Sauce

I first tasted this dish in France. In its original form, as created by the Troisgrois brothers, it was made with a butter- and cream-enriched sauce. I have eliminated the cream entirely and have reduced the butter content. Of course, it still contains 3 tablespoons of butter for four diners, so although it is lightened, it is not entirely light.

Even with the changes, it was one of Mayor Koch's favorite dishes. He told me, "If you put this sauce on sawdust, I would eat it!"

1   quart water
½   pound sorrel, about 2 bunches
4   salmon steaks or fillets, about 6 ounces each
Court Bouillon or Fish Stock (to cover salmon, about 4 cups) (see Index)
3   tablespoons cold butter

1.   Bring water to boil in large pot and blanch sorrel 1 minute. Remove and put aside.

2.   Arrange salmon in one layer in large pan. Pour in stock to cover. Bring to a simmer and poach fish until slightly underdone. (Time will depend upon the thickness of the fish.) Remove fish from stock and keep warm.

3.   Bring stock to boil and simmer until it is reduced by two-thirds. Add sorrel and mix well. Remove from heat.

4.   Add butter in small pieces, swirling the pan to incorporate butter into stock. Place salmon on plates and cover with sauce. Serve at once.

Makes 4 portions

❧ Salmon Steaks with Black Beans

I first enjoyed this dish in my favorite Chinese restaurant, Auntie Yuan, in New York. This fish is delicious served with steamed rice mixed with minced coriander. Take care not to overcook the salmon.

4 salmon steaks, about 1½ inches thick
2 red peppers, seeded and julienned
2 green peppers, seeded and julienned
4 ounces gingerroot, peeled and julienned
½ cup fermented black beans, soaked in water to cover for 3 minutes
2 cups Fish Stock (see Index)

1. Arrange salmon steaks in one layer in frying pan. Cover with peppers and ginger. Remove black beans from water and sprinkle over all. Pour stock around fish and vegetables.

2. Bring to a gentle simmer. Cover with lid or foil and simmer an additional 5-7 minutes.

3. Remove fish to a serving plate or to individual plates. Cover with vegetables. Spoon 1 tablespoon poaching liquid over each portion.

Makes 4 portions

⚜⚜ Salmon en Papillote

This dish needs no accompaniments—which is fine, because there will not be room for any on the plate. The fish will be taken from the oven slightly undercooked and will continue to cook on its own. Because the papillotes can be prepared hours ahead, refrigerated, and baked just before serving, this is an excellent dish for parties.

1   carrot, julienned
1   zucchini, julienned
1   leek, white part only, julienned
½   pound mushrooms, cut into thin slices
1   tablespoon olive oil
Freshly ground black pepper
4   salmon fillets, about 6 ounces each
4   sprigs fresh tarragon
2   tablespoons butter
4   rectangles of foil or parchment large enough to enclose fish

1.   Preheat oven to 450°F.

2.   Sauté carrot, zucchini, leek, and mushrooms in olive oil for 1 minute. Sprinkle with pepper to taste.

3.   Place 1 salmon fillet on each piece of foil. Sprinkle with pepper. Place equal amount of vegetables on top of each fish fillet. Place sprig of tarragon on top. Place ½ tablespoon butter over tarragon. Seal foil by folding the edges one over the other. Place on baking pan.

4.   Bake for 5–6 minutes. Packets will puff up. Remove and place each packet on a hot plate. Open and serve at once.

Makes 4 portions

❧   Sautéed Scallops of Salmon

1½ tablespoons olive oil
  4 scallops of salmon (have them cut very thin by fish dealer)
Salt and freshly ground black pepper
Juice of 1 lemon
  1 tablespoon chopped fresh tarragon

1. Heat oil in a heavy frying pan. Season the salmon scallops with salt and pepper to taste and cook 1 minute on each side.

2. Drain oil from the pan. Drizzle lemon juice over the salmon scallops and sprinkle with tarragon. Serve immediately.

Makes 4 portions

❧   Grilled Sardines

These small grilled fish are the ultimate in simplicity and taste. They are easy to find in the south of France, but with a little effort, you can find them in American fish markets as well. Just make sure the fish are more than 3 inches long. If they are smaller, they are not really worth preparing.

These fish are not boned before grilling. However, you can remove the backbone very easily, after you eat the top fillet.

  2 dozen fresh sardines, 3 inches or more in length
Olive oil for brushing fish
Salt
  3 lemons, cut in half
Parsley for garnish

1. Prepare a wood fire and let it burn down to embers.

2. Wash sardines and pat dry. Brush lightly with oil and season with salt to taste.

3. Grill fish 2 minutes on each side. Do not overcook.

4. Serve simply, accompanied by lemon half and parsley.

Makes 6 portions

⚜⚜⚜ Grilled Marinated Scallops of Salmon

Scallops of salmon are fast and easy to prepare. Although this dish may be seasoned with either coriander or mint leaves, I prefer the mint leaves. Marinated and grilled over a charcoal fire, they are an elegant main course. They go well with Steamed Spinach (see Index).

Juice of 1 lemon
6   tablespoons olive oil
½   cup coriander or mint leaves
Freshly ground black pepper
4   scallops of salmon

1.   Prepare a charcoal fire and let it burn to embers.

2.   Meanwhile, combine lemon juice, oil, coriander, and pepper to taste and add fish. Marinate fish for 30 minutes.

3.   Remove fish from marinade and dry with paper towels. Brush the grill rack with oil and place fish on rack. Cook 1-2 minutes and turn over, first brushing uncooked side with marinade. Grill 1 minute longer. Place on a warm plate and serve at once.

Makes 4 portions

❧ Grilled Sole

Sole's meaty texture gives it a special quality. Of all varieties, Dover sole is the most delicious, but it is also expensive and hard to find fresh in the United States. You can substitute gray or lemon sole with good results. When the fish is done, its small bones can be separated from the flesh by simply pushing them away with a spoon.

4   whole Dover sole, gray sole, or lemon sole, cleaned and skinned
       (have this done at the fish market)
Salt and freshly ground black pepper
Olive oil for brushing fish
2   lemons
2   tablespoons chopped parsley

1.   Prepare a charcoal fire and let it burn down to embers.

2.   Salt and pepper fish to taste and brush with olive oil. Place on grill for 3 minutes. Brush again with oil and turn over. Cook 3–5 minutes more.

3.   Place fish on individual plates and garnish each with ½ lemon dipped into chopped parsley.

Makes 4 portions

❧ Steamed Fillet of Sole with Duxelles, Wrapped in Spinach

I recommend that you serve this dish with Steamed Snow Peas and Carrots (see Index).

  4   large fillets of sole
Salt and freshly ground black pepper
  1   cup Duxelles (see Index)
12   large leaves spinach, blanched 5 seconds

    1.   On a work surface, lay out the fillets and season lightly with salt and pepper. Spread the Duxelles over each fillet, leaving a margin of about ¼ inch around the edges. Roll up each fillet and place seam side down on a spinach leaf. Wrap each fillet tightly in 3 spinach leaves.

    2.   Fill a pan with 2 inches water and bring to a boil. Place fish rolls on a rack above the water. Steam fish 5–7 minutes. Serve immediately.

Makes 4 portions

Variation: If you do not have a steamer rack, you can make this dish by placing the fish in a pan with ½ cup boiling water and covering the pan. Add to the water 2–3 drops lemon juice and ½ tablespoon each fresh tarragon, parsley, and thyme (or a pinch of each dried herb).

❧ Roasted Striped Bass

Crisp fennel has a natural affinity for striped bass, and I offer two recipes that combine them. In this one, the fish is stuffed with fennel; in the recipe that follows, the vegetable is prepared separately from the fish, but the two are served together.

1 whole striped bass, 4-6 pounds, cleaned (have this done at the fish market)
Salt and pepper
1 whole fennel rib
4 sprigs fresh tarragon
1 onion, peeled and chopped into large dice
1 carrot, scraped and chopped into large dice
1 fennel bulb, chopped into large dice
Olive oil for brushing

1. Preheat oven to 450°F.

2. Salt and pepper the inside of the fish to taste. Stuff with fennel rib and tarragon.

3. Arrange the roughly cut vegetables over the bottom of a roasting pan. Place the fish on the vegetables. This adds flavor and prevents the fish from sticking to the pan. Brush fish with oil; sprinkle with salt and pepper to taste.

4. Roast fish for 20-25 minutes. Remove fish from the oven and transfer to a serving platter. Discard onion and carrot. Run a large spoon down the center of the fish and push the meat away from both sides of the large center bone. Remove the bone by pulling it up. (If it doesn't move, the fish is not done.) Slice the fish into individual portions.

Makes 4-6 portions

❧ Roasted Striped Bass with Roasted Fennel

I would suggest that you make this fish for a minimum of four people; six to eight diners makes even more sense. This makes a beautiful dish for a buffet.

1   whole striped bass, 6–8 pounds, cleaned (have this done at the fish market)
Salt and freshly ground black pepper
1   medium onion, peeled and chopped into large dice
1   medium carrot, scraped and chopped into large dice
Olive oil for brushing fish
2   tablespoons olive oil
2   heads fennel, cut into quarters

1.   Preheat oven to 450°F.

2.   Salt and pepper fish inside and outside to taste. Arrange the onion and carrot over the bottom of a pan large enough to hold the fish comfortably and place fish on the bed of vegetables. This adds flavor to the fish and also prevents it from sticking to the pan. Brush with olive oil. Place in oven for 30 minutes, brushing with oil every 5 minutes.

3.   Heat the 2 tablespoons olive oil in a large frying pan and sauté fennel. Place pan of fennel in oven; do not combine fennel with fish. Roast fennel in oven for 10 minutes.

4.   To serve, remove fish from oven to large platter. Discard onion and carrot. Run a large spoon down the center of the fish and push the meat away from the center. Do this on both sides of the center bone and remove the large bone by pulling it up. Slice the fish into individual portions and serve accompanied by the roasted fennel.

Makes 6-8 portions

⚜⚜ Swordfish en Brochette

Swordfish is wonderful grilled, but it must not be overcooked. In this recipe, you sauté the mushrooms briefly first so that you will not have to overcook the fish in order to cook them through.

½   cup plus 1 tablespoon olive oil
Juice of 1 lemon
1   clove garlic, peeled and crushed
2   sprigs fresh thyme
2   pounds swordfish steaks, cut into 1-inch cubes
16   shiitake mushrooms, caps only
Salt and freshly ground black pepper

    1.   Combine ¼ cup olive oil, lemon juice, garlic, and thyme and marinate fish cubes in mixture 1 hour.

    2.   Prepare a charcoal fire and let it burn down to embers.

    3.   Heat 1 tablespoon oil in a frying pan and sauté the mushroom caps 1 minute.

    4.   Thread fish and mushroom caps on four skewers.

    5.   Place on grill and brown on all sides, about 1 minute each side. Don't overcook. Brush often with marinade during grilling. Season to taste with salt and freshly ground black pepper.

Makes 4 portions

Variation: Add 2 Roasted Peppers (see Index), cut into 1-inch cubes, to the skewers along with the fish and mushrooms.

❧❧❧ Trout with Lemon and Butter

Unlike most of the dishes in this section, trout prepared in this fashion is quite rich. One tablespoon of butter used to sauté the fish is discarded, but additional butter is added for the sauce. It comes out to about 1 tablespoon per person, so plan the rest of your menu accordingly.

¼ cup milk
2 tablespoons flour
4 medium trout, cleaned, with head and tail left on
½ tablespoon safflower oil
5 tablespoons butter
Salt and freshly ground black pepper
Juice of ½ lemon
¼ cup chopped parsley leaves

1. Preheat oven to 400°F.

2. Place milk in one shallow bowl and flour in another. Dip fish first in milk and then in flour.

3. Heat oil and 1 tablespoon of the butter in frying pan and cook fish until golden brown on both sides. Season to taste with salt and pepper.

4. Place pan in oven 2–3 minutes to finish cooking.

5. Remove fish and keep warm. Pour off fat from pan and wipe pan dry.

6. Place the remaining 4 tablespoons butter in pan over medium heat. When butter begins to brown, add lemon juice and parsley. Remove from heat, add fish, and spoon butter over. Serve immediately.

Makes 4 portions

❧❧ Grilled Marinated Tuna

Ratatouille (see Index) is an excellent accompaniment to this dish.

¼ cup olive oil
Juice of 1 lemon
2 cloves garlic, peeled and crushed
2 sprigs fresh thyme
4 pieces tuna, about 1 inch thick and 8 ounces each
Salt and freshly ground black pepper

1. Combine oil, lemon juice, garlic, and thyme and marinate fish in the mixture 1 hour.

2. Make a wood or charcoal fire and let it burn down to embers.

3. Remove fish from marinade and place directly on grill. Do not dry off marinade. Fish should be close enough to fire to become crisp. Cook 2 minutes and turn, brushing with marinade. Cook another 3 minutes and remove from heat. Be careful not to overcook, because tuna can get especially dry. Season with salt and pepper to taste. Serve at once.

Makes 4 portions

Shellfish

Steamed Littleneck Clams with Garlic and Parsley

Steamed Littleneck Clams with Pesto

Mussels Provençale

Mussels in White Wine

Asparagus with Grilled Shrimp

Shrimp with Coriander

Steamed Shrimp with Ginger

Broiled Lobster with Lemon Butter

Scallops and Oysters en Papillote with Thyme

Steamed Scallops in Spinach Leaves, on a Bed of Roasted Peppers

Scallop Brochettes

Grilled Scallops

Sautéed Scallops with Red and Yellow Peppers

I didn't serve a lot of shellfish at Gracie Mansion. Lobster and shrimp are very expensive, which makes them impractical for large-scale entertaining. But, like other costly foods, they certainly can be prepared at home for small parties.

They are special-occasion food, and I include some excellent recipes below. Lobster is magnificent when steamed or broiled. Shrimp is delicious sautéed, grilled, or steamed. It combines well with herbs such as coriander or vegetables such as asparagus.

Which brings us to mussels. People either love them or hate them, and since I love them, I try to present them at their best. In addition to the recipes that follow, please try these incomparable soups: Pureed Mussel Soup and Mussel Soup with Saffron (see Index).

When you are shopping, look for mussels that smell sweet and are not slimy. They should not be wide open. The small mussels are sweeter and more tender than the large. Try to buy cultivated mussels, which require less cleaning than the wild. They must still be scrubbed to remove barnacles, however.

I tried to serve mussels quite a bit because Mayor Koch enjoyed them. They are inexpensive and low in calories, and they are delicious with lots of garlic. (By now I think my criteria for choosing foods have become clear.)

In the south of France, mussels are simply steamed in white wine with shallots. Or they are steamed in a sauce of fresh tomatoes, onions, garlic, olives, and white wine. Served with the freshest French or Italian bread and a beautiful salad of greens, they become the perfect simple summer meal. A dessert of ripe berries is the best finale. Foods like this don't need to be fussed over or disguised. They are so natural and inviting, they cannot be improved upon.

Clams, like mussels, are best simply steamed and served with a lot of garlic. They are also low in calories and price and wonderful in soups. (Try our superb Manhattan Clam Chowder, see Index.)

When buying shellfish, be sure that their shells are tightly closed and that they smell fresh. Buy live lobsters and crabs. Shrimps have usually been frozen, and scallops are sold already shucked, so it is important that you can trust your fish dealer to sell you the best quality.

❦❦ Steamed Littleneck Clams with Garlic and Parsley

I introduced this dish to Gracie Mansion shortly before I left in November 1988. It is simple and fantastic. You can lighten or enrich it, since it is delicious with or without butter added at the end.

4 dozen littleneck clams in shells
Water for steaming clams
4 cloves garlic, peeled and mashed
4 tablespoons chopped parsley
3 tablespoons cold butter (optional)

1. Wash clams thoroughly in cold water to remove sand. Place in large pot and add ½ inch water. Cover pot and bring water to boil. Clams will steam open; discard any that do not open.

2. Combine garlic and parsley. When clams have opened, add garlic and parsley mixture and butter (if desired) and steam 30 seconds more. Remove to a warm bowl and serve at once.

Makes 4 portions

❦❦❦ Steamed Littleneck Clams with Pesto

I served these clams to a well-known New York restaurateur at a small dinner at Gracie Mansion, and he thought they were outstanding. That is praise I really enjoyed.

3-4 dozen littleneck clams in shells
Water for steaming clams
¾ cup Pesto (see Index)
Freshly ground black pepper
½ cup grated Parmesan

1. Wash clams thoroughly in cold water to remove sand. Place in large pot and add ½ inch water. Cover pot and bring water to boil. Clams will steam open; discard any that do not open.

2. Add Pesto, pepper to taste, and cheese and toss thoroughly. Serve at once.

Makes 4 portions

❧ Mussels Provençale

This is the dish I prepared for Mayor Koch when he returned from a trip to Ireland with Cardinal O'Connor. I thought that a dish of fragrant Mussels Provençale followed by Pasta with Pesto would fill his garlic quota after a week away from home.

Serve this with French bread and provide soup spoons for the sauce.

2 tablespoons olive oil
1 medium onion, peeled and chopped into medium dice
2 cups Light Tomato Sauce (see Index)
Freshly ground black pepper
4 dozen mussels, cleaned, scrubbed, and debearded
3 cloves garlic, peeled and crushed
1 dozen Niçoise olives
1 tablespoon each minced fresh tarragon, thyme, and parsley
4 sprigs basil for garnish

1. In a large pot, heat olive oil and sauté onion until tender.

2. Add tomato sauce and 2 grinds of pepper. Cook 1 minute and mix. Add mussels in shells and garlic. Mix and cover.

3. Steam mussels until they have opened. Discard any that do not open. Immediately before serving, add olives and herbs. Divide among four individual bowls and garnish each with basil.

Makes 4 portions

❧ Mussels in White Wine

This is a good dish to have in your repertoire. It is inexpensive, quick, and tasty, and it has no salt, cream, or butter. It was on my menu at Gracie Mansion from day one, literally, since it was a part of my dinner audition for the job of chef. A good accompaniment is fresh French or garlic bread.

2 cups dry white wine
½ tablespoon whole black peppercorns
½ teaspoon dried thyme
3 tablespoons chopped shallots
4 dozen mussels, cleaned, scrubbed, and debearded
1 tablespoon chopped parsley

1. Place wine, peppercorns, thyme, and shallots in a large pot and bring to a boil. Cook 2 minutes.

2. Add mussels, cover pot, and cook until mussels open. Discard any that do not open.

3. Serve in warm bowls with juice spooned over mussels. Garnish with parsley.

Makes 4 portions

❧❧ Asparagus with Grilled Shrimp

Careful presentation is one of the secrets of this dish: it is most impressive but takes a minimum of preparation. The other secret is quick cooking over intense heat, because the shrimp must not be overcooked.

2   dozen large shrimp, with heads left on if possible
2   tablespoons melted butter mixed with 2 tablespoons olive oil
2   dozen large asparagus spears peeled to ½ inch from tip (should be
      4–5 inches long)
1   tablespoon each finely chopped fresh chives, tarragon, parsley, and
      thyme
2   cups Light Tomato Sauce (see Index)
4   sprigs parsley

1.   Prepare a wood or charcoal fire and let it burn down to embers.

2.   Leaving shrimp in shell, slice in half lengthwise. Brush flesh side with oil and butter mixture.

3.   When fire has burned down, place shrimp on grill, flesh side down, for 2 minutes. Turn and brush again and cook for 1 minute. Move shrimp to side of the grill, away from direct heat.

4.   Place asparagus on grill and brush with oil and butter mixture. Grill 2 minutes, turning once.

5.   To serve, arrange 6 shrimp in the center of each plate and circle them with 6 asparagus spears arranged like the spokes of a wheel. Place spoonsful of tomato sauce between the asparagus spears. Garnish each plate with a sprig of parsley.

Makes 4 portions

111

❧ Shrimp with Coriander

1-2 tablespoons olive oil
 2 dozen large shrimp, shelled and deveined
Salt and freshly ground black pepper
 2 cloves garlic, peeled and crushed
 ½ bunch coriander (cilantro) leaves

1. Heat oil in a heavy frying pan. Season shrimp with salt and pepper to taste and cook over medium to high heat 3-4 minutes, shaking pan.

2. Remove pan from heat and add garlic and half the coriander leaves. Mix well with shrimp and return to pan for 15-20 seconds, tossing over high heat. Serve immediately, garnished with remaining coriander leaves.

Makes 4 portions

❧ Steamed Shrimp with Ginger

This dish (hardly a new creation) was added to the Gracie Mansion menu to fit the Mayor's new diet. Since the Mayor often dined with friends in Chinese restaurants, I brought a bit of Chinese cuisine home to him. This was not a regular practice of mine, since I knew I could never, ever equal the fine Chinese food that the Mayor enjoyed so much.

I recommend serving this with steamed rice.

Water for steaming
 4 dozen large shrimp, shelled and deveined
 ½ cup julienned fresh gingerroot
 2 carrots, julienned
 ¾ pound snow peas, strings removed, julienned
 4 sprigs coriander (cilantro) for garnish

1. Pour water into a steamer or large pot to a depth of 3 inches and bring to a boil.

2. Place shrimp, ginger, carrots, and snow peas in a steamer basket or colander and steam 4–5 minutes, tossing them slightly.

3. Remove from steamer and mound shrimp and vegetables on four dinner plates. Garnish with fresh coriander.

Makes 4 portions

⚜⚜⚜ Broiled Lobster with Lemon Butter

The lobsters will cook very quickly under a hot broiler. They can also be grilled, following this recipe. If the tails start to curl up, weigh them down with a heavy object. When lobsters begin to brown, move the broiler lower.

This rich dish calls for a lot of butter for two portions. However, it is used for brushing during cooking, and a good part of it will be discarded. You do not have to serve additional lemon butter with the lobster, because it will have absorbed the flavor during broiling.

5   tablespoons butter
Juice of 1 lemon
2   lobsters, 2½ pounds each, split and claws cracked (see directions in
         step 3 or have this done at the fish market)
Salt and freshly ground black pepper

1. Preheat broiler to very hot, 15–25 minutes.
2. Melt butter and combine with lemon juice.
3. Prepare lobsters: Place each lobster on its belly and insert knife in center. Run knife down the length of the lobster to split it in half. Wrap claws in a towel and crack them with a mallet or hammer.
4. Place lobsters on broiler rack shell side down. Season with salt and pepper to taste. Broil 5 minutes. Remove and brush with lemon butter. Return to broiler for 10 minutes. Remove and brush again; broil 2 additional minutes. Serve immediately.

Makes 2 portions

❧ Scallops and Oysters en Papillote with Thyme

The beautiful part of this recipe is that the individual papillotes can be prepared early in the day and refrigerated. In the evening, you can bake them just before serving, and they will take only 5 minutes. This also makes a very nice first course.

 1   dozen medium sea scallops (if large, cut in half)
 1   dozen oysters, shucked (have this done at the fish market)
Salt and freshly ground black pepper
4-8   sprigs fresh thyme or large pinch dried
 2   tablespoons butter
Olive oil for brushing (optional)
 4   rectangles of aluminum foil or parchment

1.   Preheat oven to 450°F.

2.   Set out four sheets of parchment or foil. Place 3 scallops and 3 oysters in the center of each sheet. Season with salt and pepper to taste. Place 1 or 2 sprigs of fresh thyme or pinch of dried thyme on top of scallops and oysters and top with ½ tablespoon butter. Tightly fold up the edges of the foil or parchment, sealing it into a packet. If using parchment, brush the outside of each packet with a little oil.

3.   Bake 5 minutes. Serve the individual packets, letting your guests open them at the table.

Makes 4 portions

⚜ Steamed Scallops in Spinach Leaves, on a Bed of Roasted Peppers

There was a time when I would eat only the small bay scallops. However, I have since come to appreciate the excellent flavor of sea scallops.

4   cups water
1   teaspoon salt
16   large spinach leaves
16   large sea scallops
Salt and freshly ground black pepper
1   cup Fish Stock (see Index)
4   Roasted Peppers (see Index)
½   tablespoon olive oil

1.   Boil water with salt added. Blanch spinach leaves in salted water for 10 seconds.

2.   Spread leaves on a work surface and place 1 scallop on each leaf, season with salt and pepper to taste, and wrap up, placing seam side down.

3.   Place Fish Stock in a large sauté pan and bring to a simmer. Place scallops in pan, cover pan, and cook at medium heat 4–5 minutes.

4.   Meanwhile, julienne roasted peppers. Heat ½ tablespoon oil in a frying pan and sauté peppers 1 minute. Season lightly with salt and pepper.

5.   Divide peppers among four dinner plates and cover each portion with 4 scallops.

Makes 4 portions

❧ Scallop Brochettes

In this delicate dish the scallops are flavored by the lemon zests placed next to them on barbecue skewers. A good accompaniment is steamed rice flavored with thyme. Simply mix 1 tablespoon chopped fresh thyme into 2 cups steamed rice.

2 medium vidalia onions, peeled and blanched
Zest of two lemons, with no white membrane attached
12 shiitake mushrooms, caps only
1½ pounds large sea scallops
Olive oil for brushing
Salt and freshly ground black pepper

1. Prepare a wood or charcoal fire and let it burn down to embers. Or preheat broiler.

2. Cut onions into quarters. Cut lemon zests into ¼-inch strips.

3. On four skewers, thread vegetables alternately with scallops and zests.

4. Grill or broil, brushing with olive oil, 4–5 minutes. Turn once. Salt and pepper to taste.

Makes 4 portions

Variation: Add large, peeled garlic cloves to the skewers.

✿ Grilled Scallops

This delicious dish could not be easier to prepare. Buy scallops that are large enough to sit on the grill without falling through. If you like, you can thread them on skewers, but this is not really necessary. Serve with Light Tomato Sauce and Parsley Steamed Potatoes (see Index).

2 pounds large sea scallops
2 tablespoons oil
Salt and freshly ground black pepper
2 tablespoons fresh thyme, slightly minced

1. Prepare a wood or charcoal fire and let it burn down to embers.

2. Brush scallops with oil and season lightly with salt and pepper. Place directly on grill. Cook 1–2 minutes; brush with oil; turn and cook an additional 2 minutes. Sprinkle with thyme during last minute of grilling.

Makes 4 portions

⚜ Sautéed Scallops with Red and Yellow Peppers

This dish is excellent accompanied by steamed rice or Parsley Steamed Potatoes (see Index).

2 tablespoons olive oil
1½ pounds sea scallops
1 medium yellow pepper, julienned
1 medium red pepper, julienned
1 clove garlic, peeled and crushed
Salt and freshly ground black pepper
1 tablespoon fresh tarragon leaves (*or* ¼ tablespoon dried)

1. Heat oil in a frying pan. Add scallops and sauté 1 minute. Remove from pan.

2. Add peppers and sauté until tender, 2–3 minutes. Add garlic to pan and cook garlic 1 minute, taking care not to burn.

3. Return scallops to pan. Add salt and pepper to taste and tarragon leaves. Toss over high heat. Serve immediately.

Makes 4 portions

Chicken

Roasted Chicken with Black Peppercorns

Roasted Chicken with Thirty-Five Cloves of Garlic

Broiled Chicken

Chicken Sautéed with Fresh Herbs

Chicken Stuffed Under the Skin with Farmer Cheese

Chicken Breasts Stuffed with Duxelles

Chicken Breasts with Balsamic Vinegar

Chicken Cutlets with Rosemary

Chicken Breasts with Wild Mushrooms and Persillade

Chicken Scallops Sautéed with Mint

Sautéed Chicken with Pesto

Chicken is versatile, delicious, readily available, easy to prepare, and popular with almost everyone. To me and to many other chefs, a perfectly roasted chicken is the ideal meal. As I said earlier, when I prepare a special treat for myself, it is likely to consist of Roasted Chicken (with plenty of crushed black peppercorns) and Caesar Salad (see Index).

Chicken is adaptable to many preparations hot and cold. Whole chickens can be roasted, grilled, steamed, or poached. Chicken parts can be sautéed, grilled, roasted, or broiled. Skinless, boneless breasts are superb when pounded and grilled and served with a salad of arugula and tomatoes, exactly as one would serve the more expensive veal. Numerous vegetables, sauces, and herbs can enhance chicken, or it can be served in unadorned perfection.

So what is wrong with chicken? Only this: it seems to have a reputation for being budget fare. Upscale chickens—poussins and the like—have been presented to the American public and have glorified the chicken's image. Poussins are all right if you don't mind a lot of little bones. Cornish hens are a lot of trouble to dissect. Free range chickens are expensive, and I don't find them superior to the best fresh chickens I buy from my local market.

❦❦ Roasted Chicken with Black Peppercorns

Here, in my opinion, is the recipe that produces the perfect roasted chicken. Don't forget to baste often—basting and roasting at a high temperature are the crucial steps in preparation.

One chicken serves two people generously. You can double the recipe for more guests.

1   chicken, 2½–3 pounds
Kosher salt
1   tablespoon black peppercorns, crushed
2   tablespoons butter or olive oil
1   bunch watercress for garnish
Kitchen string for tying the legs

1.   Preheat oven to 450°F.

2.   Rub the inside of the chicken with kosher salt to taste. Crush peppercorns by placing the flat blade of a knife over them and pounding with your hand. Sprinkle crushed peppercorns over outside of chicken, along with some salt. Tie chicken legs together.

3.   Heat butter or oil in a cast-iron pan large enough to hold the chicken. Turn chicken in oil over medium heat. Set chicken on its side and place in oven 15 minutes. Turn on other side and roast 15 minutes. Turn oven down to 400°F. Place chicken on its back and roast 25–30 minutes, basting with pan juices every 5 minutes.

4.   Remove from oven and carve. Garnish with watercress.

Makes 2 portions

122

❦❦ Roasted Chicken with Thirty-Five Cloves of Garlic

The garlic, roasted with the chicken, has a sweet flavor and is not at all harsh. Begin basting only after you have turned the chicken onto its back; that is, after it has roasted about 30 minutes.

1 chicken, 2½–3 pounds
Kosher salt
2 tablespoons butter or olive oil
35 cloves garlic, unpeeled
1 bunch watercress for garnish
Kitchen string for tying the legs

1. Preheat oven to 450°F.

2. Rub cavity of chicken with salt and sprinkle skin lightly with salt. Tie legs together.

3. Heat butter or oil in a cast-iron pan large enough to hold the chicken. Turn chicken in butter over medium heat. Place chicken on its side and roast 15 minutes. Turn on other side and roast 15 minutes. Pour fat out of pan. Turn oven down to 400°F. Place chicken on its back and surround it with the cloves of garlic. Continue roasting for 30–35 minutes, basting every 5 minutes.

4. Remove from oven and carve into serving pieces. Serve surrounded by watercress and sprinkled with garlic cloves.

Makes 4 portions

123

❦❦   Broiled Chicken

This chicken has to be done at the last minute, and it will require a lot of attention. The chicken requires a very hot broiler, and you must take care to avoid burning. Nevertheless, it is one of my favorite things to eat, and I offer generous portions.

Three tablespoons of butter are called for to serve four people. Serve hot with Steamed Spinach (see Index). You can also serve the next day, after allowing the chicken to come to room temperature.

2   chickens, 2½–3 pounds each, cut in halves
Salt and freshly ground black pepper
3   tablespoons butter, melted

    1.   Preheat broiler for 15–25 minutes, until very hot.
    2.   Salt and pepper the chickens lightly. Place chicken 2 inches from the heat, skin side up. When chicken starts to brown, begin basting with a small amount of butter. Continue cooking for 10 minutes. Turn chicken and repeat process, being careful that the chicken does not burn. Broil 20–25 minutes.

Makes 4 portions

Variation: Ten minutes before the chicken is done, turn it skin side down. Sprinkle with ¼ cup rosemary leaves combined with 2 cloves garlic, peeled and minced. Baste with 2 tablespoons melted butter and complete broiling, turning once. The garlic and herb flavor will permeate the chicken.

❧❧ Chicken Sautéed with Fresh Herbs

This was a good dish to serve at Gracie Mansion, because I could add as much garlic as I wanted to. It also illustrates my favorite kind of cooking: it is simple and quick, and it uses fresh herbs for flavoring.

2   chickens, 2½–3 pounds each
Salt and freshly ground black pepper
2   tablespoons olive oil
Juice of 1 lemon
3   cloves garlic, peeled and diced
1   cup mixed fresh thyme, tarragon, chives, and basil (if you use
       rosemary as well, use a small amount because it tends to
       overwhelm the other herbs)
2   tablespoons cold butter, cut into bits

1.   Cut chickens into eighths. Sprinkle with salt and pepper to taste. Heat olive oil in a heavy pan large enough to hold the chicken without crowding or use two pans. Brown chicken well on all sides (about 30 minutes), beginning with the dark meat and adding the light meat pieces later.

2.   Add lemon juice and garlic and cook 30 seconds.

3.   Remove pan from heat. Add herbs and butter, toss, and serve at once.

Makes 4–6 portions

125

✿✿✿ Chicken Stuffed Under the Skin with Farmer Cheese

This is my version of the wonderful dish created by the famous chef, Michel Guérard. It is undoubtedly rich and best served with light accompaniments. In the Introduction, I give a menu built around this chicken that will help you to balance its richness.

When stuffing the chicken, be especially careful not to break the skin.

1   chicken, about 3½ pounds
Salt and freshly ground black pepper
1   pound farmer cheese
2   tablespoons each minced fresh chervil, chives, and tarragon
1   tablespoon minced fresh rosemary
1   egg, slightly beaten
2   tablespoons olive oil
2   tablespoons melted butter
Kitchen string for tying the legs

1.   Preheat oven to 425°F.

2.   Sprinkle inside of chicken with salt and pepper to taste. Loosen skin from breast and as much of thighs as possible.

3.   Combine cheese, herbs, and egg and mix well. Stuff chicken under the skin with cheese mixture. Tie chicken legs together (it is not necessary to truss the entire bird).

4.   Brush chicken with olive oil and place in heavy pan with lid. Place in oven and cook covered, 1 hour.

5.   Remove from oven and brush chicken with butter. Put back in oven uncovered and roast an additional 25–30 minutes, basting frequently with pan juices.

Makes 4 portions

⚜⚜ Chicken Breasts Stuffed with Duxelles

This dish is fancy but fast.

2   large chicken breasts, cut into halves and boned
1   cup Duxelles (see Index)
Salt and freshly ground black pepper
2   tablespoons olive oil, plus a small amount for brushing
½   cup dry white wine
½   cup Chicken Stock (see Index)
½   cup mixed fresh thyme, rosemary, and tarragon

1.   Preheat oven to 400°F.

2.   Separate most of the skin from the chicken flesh and stuff the Duxelles under the skin evenly. Sprinkle the chicken breasts with salt and pepper to taste.

3.   Heat oil in a heavy ovenproof pan and brown chicken quickly, skin side down. Turn over chicken breasts and brush lightly with olive oil. Place pan in oven and bake 10 minutes.

4.   Remove pan from oven and place over high heat. Add wine and reduce by two-thirds. Add Chicken Stock and again reduce by two-thirds. Remove pan from heat and add herbs. To serve, spoon sauce over each portion.

Makes 4 portions

❧❧ Chicken Breasts with Balsamic Vinegar

The delicious sauce made from the cooking juices and the balsamic vinegar is somewhat strong. Spoon only a small amount over the chicken or onto the plate.

2   chicken breasts, cut into halves, skinned, and boned
1   tablespoon butter
2   tablespoons olive oil
¼   cup balsamic vinegar
2   tablespoons chopped parsley

   1.   Pound chicken breasts thin. Heat butter in frying pan with 1 tablespoon of the olive oil and add chicken. Sauté until brown; turn and brown other side.

   2.   Remove pan from heat. Combine the remaining 1 tablespoon oil and vinegar and add to pan. Sprinkle chicken with parsley and serve immediately.

Makes 4 portions

❧❧ Chicken Cutlets with Rosemary

I find steamed vegetables make a beautiful contrast to the sautéed chicken and are a good foil for the rather strong flavor of rosemary.

   This is another dish where the flavor of butter is important, although only 3 tablespoons are used for four people.

4   large or 8 small chicken breast cutlets
Salt and freshly ground black pepper
Flour for dusting
3   tablespoons butter
3   tablespoons fresh rosemary

   1.   Pound chicken cutlets until thin. Sprinkle with salt and pepper to taste. Dust lightly with flour.

   2.   Heat butter in a large, heavy frying pan. Brown chicken cutlets on both sides. When browned, add rosemary to pan and toss. Serve at once.

Makes 4 portions

❧❧ Chicken Breasts with Wild Mushrooms and Persillade

This simple dish is excellent served with Steamed Spinach or a Mélange of Steamed Vegetables (see Index).

2   chicken breasts, cut into halves, bone in
Salt and freshly ground black pepper
2   tablespoons olive oil
1   pound wild mushrooms (chanterelles, morels, or cepes), washed,
        stems removed, and caps cut in half if large
½   cup Persillade (see Index)

1.   Sprinkle chicken with salt and pepper to taste. Heat olive oil in a frying pan and brown chicken on one side. Turn and add mushrooms to pan.

2.   Sauté 7–8 minutes or until chicken is firm, shaking pan or turning chicken to avoid burning.

3.   When chicken is done, remove pan from heat and add Persillade. The Persillade should not be cooked except from the heat of the pan. Serve at once.

Makes 4 portions

❧❧ Chicken Scallops Sautéed with Mint

This dish is excellent served with Steamed Zucchini and Carrots (see Index).

2   chicken breasts, cut into halves, skinned, and boned
Salt and freshly ground black pepper
¼   cup flour
2   tablespoons butter
1   tablespoon olive oil
¼   cup fresh mint leaves
½   lemon, squeezed

    1.   Pound each half breast thin and cut into three pieces. Season with salt and pepper to taste and lightly dredge in flour.

    2.   Heat butter and olive oil in a frying pan and brown chicken pieces, turning once. When chicken is golden brown, add mint and lemon juice to pan and toss 10 seconds. Serve at once.

Makes 4 portions

❧❧❧ Sautéed Chicken with Pesto

This garlic- and basil-rich dish was a natural for Mayor Koch. It's delicious served with Sautéed Cherry Tomatoes (see Index).

2   tablespoons olive oil
2   chicken breasts, cut into halves, bone in
Salt and freshly ground black pepper
½–¾   cup Pesto (see Index)
3   tablespoons water or Chicken Stock (see Index)

    1.   Heat oil in a frying pan large enough to hold the chicken without crowding. Sprinkle chicken breasts with salt and pepper to taste. Cook slowly over medium heat to avoid overbrowning. Turn often. When done, chicken should be a deep golden color.

    2.   Thin Pesto with water or stock. Remove pan from heat and toss chicken with Pesto.

Makes 4 portions

Veal

Veal Medallions with Morels

Veal Scalloppine with Coriander

Veal Scalloppine with Calvados, Garnished with Glazed Apples

Veal Chops Arugula

Roasted Veal Chops on a Bed of Leeks and Mushrooms

Veal Chops with Red and Yellow Peppers

Broiled Veal Chops with Artichokes

Osso Buco

Pot Roast of Veal with Pearl Onions

Braised Veal with Onions

Veal was not exactly a staple of my Gracie Mansion kitchen, nor is it at many large dinner parties, because it is expensive. However, it does make an elegant meal for a small, special party. It is easy to prepare, tender, and appealing to most diners.

Veal scallops and medallions cook very quickly and are easy to prepare. Scallops are ¼-inch slices cut from the leg and pounded paper thin. Medallions are ¾-inch slices from the loin that are pounded with the heel of the hand or placed between sheets of waxed paper and pounded with a rolling pin to a thickness of ½ inch.

Because scallops and medallions are so thin, you must guard against overcooking them. Cook them quickly so they do not dry out. These cuts must be prepared at the last minute and served immediately.

Sautéing is the best and easiest way to cook them. Make sure the oil is very hot, and flour and season scallops at the last second before cooking. You need not flour medallions. Brown the veal scallops over high heat for about 1 minute; cook medallions slightly longer. Turn and brown the second side. When the second side is browned, the veal is done. You now have the beginning of many elegant recipes. The sautéed veal marries beautifully with morels, domestic mushrooms, ginger, coriander, peppers, or glazed apples, as you will see in the following recipes.

Veal chops are also delicious. I prefer the rib to the loin because it is more pleasing to the eye and makes a better presentation. Chops should be 1½ inches thick so that they don't dry out when grilled, broiled, or pan fried. Veal chops are marvelous with no further garnish when properly cooked. However, they are superlative broiled and served with artichokes or on a bed of braised leeks. They are absolutely heavenly when pounded thin, grilled, and topped with a salad of arugula and tomatoes.

This section includes the recipe that started my career at Gracie Mansion, the rich, garlicky Osso Buco. I offer it with my blessings to anyone seeking work as a chef.

⚜⚜ Veal Medallions with Morels

This is a luxury dish, and I prepared it only two or three times at Gracie Mansion. It is festive and would be perfect for a special, small dinner party, perhaps on New Year's Eve.

3   tablespoons olive oil
⅓   cup minced shallots
1   pound fresh morels (cut in halves if large)
¼   cup dry white wine
½   cup Brown Veal Stock (see Index)
Salt and freshly ground black pepper
1½   pounds veal medallions, pounded thin
Chopped parsley for garnish

    1.   Heat 1 tablespoon of the oil in large pan. Sauté shallots until soft but not brown. Add morels and sauté 1 minute. Add wine and simmer until wine is reduced by two-thirds. Add veal stock and simmer 3 minutes. Add salt and pepper to taste.

    2.   In another pan, heat remaining 2 tablespoons oil. Sauté veal medallions until lightly browned on each side. If pan is not large enough to fit all the veal without crowding, sauté in two batches. Pour off fat; wipe out pan with paper towel.

    3.   Return veal to pan. Add morel sauce and cook over high heat 2 minutes. Garnish with chopped parsley. Serve at once.

Makes 4 portions

🌿🌿 Veal Scalloppine with Coriander

This elegant entree can be prepared in 15 minutes from start to finish. In fact, if you take longer, you are doing something wrong. Your secret is the veal stock, which stands ready in your freezer.

  1 pound veal scallops, pounded thin
Salt and freshly ground black pepper
  2 tablespoons flour for dredging
  3 tablespoons olive oil
¼–½ cup Brown Veal Stock (see Index)
  ¼ cup fresh coriander (cilantro) leaves, well washed

1. Salt and pepper veal scallops to taste and flour lightly.

2. In a large pan, heat oil until very hot. Arrange veal in pan in one layer. Brown and turn once to brown other side. This should take 3–4 minutes.

3. When second side is browned, add veal stock. Reduce over high heat by one-half.

4. Remove from heat and add coriander leaves.

5. Place scallops on individual plates. Cover with coriander sauce and serve at once.

Makes 4 portions

❧❧ Veal Scalloppine with Calvados, Garnished with Glazed Apples

Veal is often combined with sherry, but I find Calvados more interesting (I also hate sherry). It jazzes up a simple dish and turns it into a festive main course. This is perfect for an intimate Christmas or New Year's dinner for four.

Glazed Apples
2   Granny Smith apples
¼   cup water
1   tablespoon sugar
1   tablespoon cold butter, cut into bits

Veal
1   pound veal scallops, pounded thin
4   tablespoons flour
3   tablespoons butter
¼   cup Calvados
¼   cup Brown Veal Stock (see Index)
2   tablespoons chopped parsley

1. Preheat oven to 375°F.
2. Peel and core apples. Slice ¼ inch thick.
3. Place apples in ovenproof pan. Add water. Sprinkle with sugar and butter.
4. Bake apples until brown and glazed, about 5–10 minutes.
5. When apples are done, dredge veal scallops in flour.
6. Melt butter in a large, heavy pan. Add veal and brown over medium-high heat. Turn scallops and brown other side.
7. Add Calvados to pan. Raise heat and cook until Calvados is reduced by two-thirds.
8. Add veal stock and cook over high heat 2 minutes. Add parsley.
9. Serve immediately, garnished with glazed apples.

Makes 4 portions

136

❦❦ Veal Chops Arugula

This dish is often prepared by breading and sautéing the chops before topping them with salad. I think my grilled version is much more interesting, as well as fun to make and fun to eat. The flavors and textures go together well, and grilled chops are especially light.

4   veal chops, about 1¼ inches thick
Salt and freshly ground black pepper
Olive oil for brushing veal chops
1   large red onion, sliced
2   medium tomatoes, diced
2   bunches arugula, well washed
Juice of 1 lemon
¼   cup olive oil for salad

1.   Prepare a wood or charcoal fire and let it burn down to embers.

2.   Place each veal chop between sheets of waxed paper and flatten with rolling pin to ¼ inch thick. Season with salt and pepper to taste.

3.   Brush chops with olive oil and grill 2 minutes on each side.

4.   Combine sliced onions and diced tomatoes. Tear arugula into small pieces and toss with the other vegetables. Set aside.

5.   Mix lemon juice and olive oil and toss with arugula salad. (This must be done at the last minute.)

6.   Place each chop on an individual plate and cover with a mound of salad. Serve at once.

Makes 4 portions

⚜⚜ Roasted Veal Chops on a Bed of Leeks and Mushrooms

A high oven temperature is essential for roasting. This method of roasting vegetables is simple but adds a unique flavor to the dish.

3   tablespoons olive oil
2   bunches leeks, cleaned well and cut roughly into thirds
1   pound shiitake mushrooms
8   cloves garlic, unpeeled
4   leaves fresh sage
Freshly ground black pepper
4   veal chops, about 1½ inches thick

1. Preheat oven to 500°F.

2. Heat 2 tablespoons of the oil in a sauté pan. Add leeks and sauté 3–4 minutes. Add mushrooms, garlic, and sage. Sauté 2–3 minutes over high heat. Grind fresh black pepper to taste over the vegetables.

3. In a separate pan, heat remaining 1 tablespoon oil. Brown chops on both sides.

4. Place the vegetables in an ovenproof gratin dish or pan. Place the browned chops on top of the bed of vegetables.

5. Turn the oven down to 450°F. Roast the veal and vegetables for 10 minutes.

6. To serve, place a chop in the center of each plate and cover with the vegetable mixture.

Makes 4 portions

❧❧❧ Veal Chops with Red and Yellow Peppers

Red and yellow peppers add color and texture to a dish of simple veal chops, and balsamic vinegar provides an interesting flavor contrast.

You can grill these chops instead of sautéing them and cut down on the amount of olive oil needed. This will change the rating to moderate.

    4   rib veal chops, about 1½ inches thick
Salt and freshly ground black pepper
    5   tablespoons olive oil
    2   Roasted (Red) Peppers (see Index)
    2   Roasted (Yellow) Peppers (see Index)
  4-8   fresh basil leaves for garnish
    1   tablespoon balsamic vinegar

1. Lightly salt and pepper veal chops.

2. Heat 2 tablespoons of the olive oil in large pan and sauté chops quickly, browning on both sides. This should take about 4-7 minutes. Remove chops from pan and set aside.

3. In 1 tablespoon olive oil, sauté peppers quickly (about 1-2 minutes).

4. Arrange the peppers on four individual dinner plates. Place 1 chop on each plate on top of the peppers. Garnish with basil leaves.

5. Combine remaining 2 tablespoons olive oil and the balsamic vinegar and drizzle over the veal and peppers.

Makes 4 portions

Variation: Prepare a wood or charcoal fire and let it burn down to embers. Brush chops with olive oil and season with salt and pepper. Grill chops 3-4 minutes on each side, slightly longer if chops are thicker. When done, top with sautéed peppers, as above.

❧❧❧ Broiled Veal Chops with Artichokes

If I were making this for Mayor Koch, I would definitely add 4 cloves of garlic. They go well with the veal and artichokes, although the dish is equally excellent without them.

2   veal chops from the rack, about 1½ inches thick
2   tablespoons olive oil
Salt and freshly ground black pepper
4   large artichokes, trimmed down to the heart
Water for cooking artichoke hearts
4   cloves garlic, peeled and crushed (optional)

1.   Preheat broiler.

2.   Brush chops with 1 tablespoon olive oil and season with salt and pepper to taste. Place under broiler and broil 3-4 minutes on each side.

3.   While chops are broiling, simmer artichoke hearts in water to cover, 8-10 minutes.

4.   Remove artichoke hearts from water, slice thinly, and sauté in remaining 1 tablespoon olive oil for 1 minute, with garlic, if desired.

5.   Place hot chops on plates, season with freshly ground pepper, and cover with sautéed artichoke hearts.

Makes 2 portions

❧ Osso Buco

Here it is! This is the simple yet unforgettable recipe that won me the job of Gracie Mansion chef. Be sure to have on hand your best veal stock, fresh or defrosted.

4   pieces veal shank (have butcher cut into 1½-inch pieces)
½   cup flour
Salt and freshly ground black pepper
2   tablespoons olive oil
3   large onions, julienned
1   cup white wine
3   cups Brown Veal Stock (see Index)
Rind of 1 lemon
Juice of 1 lemon
4   anchovy fillets
½   cup chopped parsley
4   cloves garlic, peeled and chopped

1.   Preheat oven to 400°F.

2.   Dredge veal shanks with flour. Salt and pepper to taste.

3.   Heat oil in roasting pan over medium heat. Brown shanks on all sides. Remove from pan and set aside.

4.   Add onions to pan and brown well over medium heat.

5.   Return veal to roasting pan and add wine. Reduce wine by one-half over high heat. Add veal stock and cook over high heat for 4 minutes.

6.   Cover tightly and cook in oven for 1 hour. Remove from oven. Veal should be very tender; if not, return to oven for 15 minutes.

7.   Chop together all remaining ingredients to make parsley sauce. Place some of the mixture on each piece of veal. Cover and return to oven for about 1 minute.

8.   Remove from oven. Place one piece of veal on each plate and surround with onions and sauce. Serve immediately.

Makes 4 portions

❧ Pot Roast of Veal with Pearl Onions

This was not one of the Mayor's favorites, but I'm happy to say it is one of mine. Veal makes a delicious pot roast that is much lighter than beef. I think the dish probably didn't suit the Mayor because it is missing an important ingredient—garlic. But I felt that garlic would completely overwhelm the flavor of the veal and vegetables.

Be sure to brown the meat well—browning is an important step in this recipe. This dish is delicious accompanied by Steamed Haricots Verts (see Index).

3   tablespoons olive oil
2   ribs celery, sliced thin
2   medium onions, peeled and sliced
2   dozen pearl onions, peeled
2   carrots, scraped and sliced
1   boned veal roast, about 3 pounds
2   medium tomatoes, peeled and chopped
1   Bouquet Garni (see Index)
2   cups dry white wine

1.   Preheat oven to 325°F.

2.   Heat oil in a large ovenproof pan and brown celery, onions, and carrots. Add veal to pan and brown on all sides.

3.   Add tomatoes, Bouquet Garni, and wine. Bring to a boil, lower to a simmer, and cover pan.

4.   Place in oven and cook for 1½ hours. Test for doneness by piercing with a sharp knife. Veal should be very tender.

5.   Slice veal and serve with pan juices. Garnish with pearl onions.

Makes 6 portions

❧ Braised Veal with Onions

This fragrant dish is a welcome dinner on a cold winter or fall night.

1   tablespoon olive oil
1   medium onion, sliced thin
1   rolled veal roast, about 3 pounds
2   carrots, scraped and sliced thin
2   ribs celery, sliced thin
2   medium tomatoes, peeled and chopped
Salt and freshly ground black pepper
2   cups white wine

1. Preheat oven to 350°F.

2. Heat olive oil in a roasting pan and sauté onion until lightly browned. Add veal roast and brown well on all sides. Add remaining vegetables and season meat and vegetables with salt and pepper to taste.

3. Add wine and bring to a simmer. Cover pot. Place in oven for 1½ hours.

4. To serve, remove veal from pot and cut into ¼-inch slices. Remove grease from top of sauce and discard. Stir the sauce to distribute the vegetables. Place two slices of veal on each dinner plate and top with sauce, making sure to include the vegetables.

Makes 6 portions

Lamb and Beef

Rack of Lamb

Medallions of Lamb with Green Peppercorns

Medallions of Lamb with Wild Mushrooms

Lamb Curry with Apples

Leg of Lamb with Vegetables in One Pot

Roast Leg of Lamb

Grilled Butterflied Leg of Lamb

Leftover Lamb Patties with Yogurt and Parsley Sauce

Marinated Flank Steak

Poached Fillet of Beef with Horseradish Sauce and
Roasted Vegetables

Fillet Steak au Poivre

Beef Stew with Winter Vegetables

Although I enjoy many varieties of lamb and beef, my cuisine has moved away from red meats as it has lightened. I have included here the most practical, simple recipes for these meats, as well as a few recipes that are especially elegant.

An occasional steak, grilled or au poivre, certainly has a place in most diets. For a perfect summer dinner, all you need is a beautifully grilled fillet steak, fresh white corn on the cob, and red, juicy, sliced tomatoes. The grilled Marinated Flank Steak also makes an excellent summer meal.

My recipe for Leg of Lamb with Vegetables in One Pot is an indispensable addition to every cook's repertoire; it served me well over the years in Gracie Mansion. The Roast Leg of Lamb, while simple, can be impressive enough for your most important guests.

The recipe for Poached Fillet of Beef is not traditional; the fillet is simmered in broth and served accompanied by roasted vegetables and horseradish and yogurt sauce. A traditional horseradish sauce contains sour cream; this one is improved by the substitution of yogurt. To lighten dinner further, surround the beef with steamed vegetables, rather than roasted ones. The yogurt sauce enhances both the beef and the vegetables.

Both the Rack of Lamb and the Medallions of Lamb with Green Peppercorns are company fare—I served the latter at a very special dinner for the king and queen of Sweden. Lamb medallions are also luxurious prepared with wild mushrooms.

Finally, I include Beef Stew with Winter Vegetables, a favorite of mine. Everyone needs a truly comforting meal sometimes, and this is it.

❧❧ Rack of Lamb

This is truly a luxurious meal reserved for the most special guests. I give quantities for two people, which can be doubled or tripled if you wish. This dish is wonderful served with tiny Steamed Haricots Verts or pristine Steamed Spinach (see Index). In other words, it doesn't need enhancing.

When you buy the lamb, be sure to tell your butcher to remove excess fat from the top.

1   rack of lamb, trimmed
2   cloves garlic, peeled and slivered
Salt and freshly ground black pepper
2   tablespoons dried thyme
1   tablespoon olive oil

1.   Preheat oven to 375°F.

2.   Make small cuts in the fatty side of the rack of lamb and insert garlic slivers. Sprinkle lamb with salt, pepper, and thyme. Rub seasonings well into lamb.

3.   Heat olive oil over medium-high heat. Place lamb in pan fat side down and brown. Turn lamb over and place pan in oven for 15 minutes. Lamb will be medium rare and should be served at once. For medium, cook another 5 minutes.

Makes 2 portions

✿✿ Medallions of Lamb with Green Peppercorns

This is a regal dish, prepared for the king and queen of Sweden when they visited Gracie Mansion. When served at home, Parsley Steamed Potatoes (see Index) or mashed potatoes are an excellent accompaniment.

8   medallions of lamb, cut from the loin, about 3 ounces each
Salt
2   tablespoons butter
4   shallots, peeled and mashed
½   cup white wine
1½ cups reduced Brown Veal Stock (see Index)
2   tablespoons water-packed green peppercorns, drained

1. Place lamb medallions between sheets of waxed paper and pound to a thickness of ½ inch. Salt to taste.

2. Heat butter in frying pan until very hot but be careful not to let it burn. Add lamb medallions and sauté each side 1 minute. Remove lamb from pan and keep warm.

3. Add shallots to pan and toss 5 seconds. Add white wine and reduce by two-thirds. Add reduced stock and reduce the entire mixture by one-half. Add peppercorns.

4. Place 2 medallions of lamb on each dinner plate. Pour 1 tablespoon of sauce over each. Serve immediately.

Makes 4 portions

Medallions of Lamb with Wild Mushrooms

¼ pound wild mushrooms (morels, chanterelles, or shiitake)
8 medallions of lamb, cut from the loin, about 3 ounces each
Salt and freshly ground black pepper
2 tablespoons olive oil
1 cup Brown Veal Stock (see Index)
2 tablespoons chopped parsley
4 sprigs fresh thyme

1. Rinse mushrooms under running water. Make sure all sand and grit are removed. If using morels, cut in half. If using other mushrooms, slice ¼ inch thick.

2. Place lamb medallions between sheets of waxed paper and pound to a thickness of ½ inch. Sprinkle with salt and pepper to taste.

3. Heat olive oil in a pan large enough to hold the medallions with room to spare. Brown lamb quickly over high heat, turning only once. (This will take a total of 2–3 minutes.) While lamb is browning, add mushrooms and sauté until tender.

4. Add veal stock and reduce over high heat by two-thirds. Add chopped parsley and fresh thyme. Serve at once.

Makes 4 portions

❧❧ Lamb Curry with Apples

A very small amount of butter brings out the delicious fruit taste important to this dish.

Pinch salt and freshly ground black pepper
2   tablespoons curry powder
3   pounds lamb shoulder, cubed
3   tablespoons light olive oil
1   onion, peeled and chopped
2   tablespoons flour
Water to cover
½   pound apples
2   small bananas
1   tablespoon butter

1. Preheat oven to 325°F. Mix salt, pepper, and curry powder and sprinkle over lamb.

2. In a large frying pan, heat oil and brown lamb on one side. Turn lamb and add onion, stirring often.

3. When onion has browned, sprinkle meat and onion with flour, still cooking and stirring. Take care that you do not burn the flour.

4. Add water to cover and stir to blend. Simmer and taste.

5. Cover pan, place in oven, and cook 2–2½ hours. Test for doneness by piercing meat with a knife point. Remove from oven.

6. Meanwhile, peel and quarter apples and remove seeds. Peel bananas and cut into thirds. Heat butter in a pan large enough to hold the lamb and brown the fruit. Add lamb cubes.

7. Degrease the sauce and reduce by one-third over high heat. Strain sauce and serve with meat.

Makes 6 portions

❦❦ Leg of Lamb with Vegetables in One Pot

This is a dish I often made at Gracie Mansion when a dinner party had been scheduled at the last minute. Not only is it easy to prepare, but there is very little to clean up afterwards.

Although lamb is high in fat, this preparation uses no oil and qualifies as light.

1   leg of lamb, 5–6 pounds
3   cloves garlic, peeled and cut into slivers
1   tablespoon minced fresh rosemary (*or* 1 teaspoon dried)
½   tablespoon minced fresh thyme or pinch dried
Salt and freshly ground black pepper
2   pounds Idaho potatoes, scrubbed and cut into quarters
1   dozen small white onions, peeled
6–8   medium turnips, peeled and cut into large dice
2   bunches carrots, scrubbed and cut into chunks

1.   Preheat oven to 475°F.

2.   Stud lamb with garlic slivers. Season with herbs and salt and pepper to taste.

3.   Place cut potatoes in large, heavy roasting pan. Place lamb on top of potatoes. Roast for 30 minutes.

4.   Add remaining vegetables to pan. Lower oven to 400°F and roast 30 minutes longer. Stir vegetables frequently.

5.   Remove from oven. Carve roast lamb and serve with vegetables.

Makes 8 portions

❦❦ Roast Leg of Lamb

I prepared this dish for a distinguished guest of Mayor Koch's, the governor of Cairo, Egypt. (In Egypt, a mayor has the title "governor.") I thought a lamb dish was appropriate, since lamb is prepared often in the Middle East, but I also thought this one had a distinctly American flavor.

1   leg of lamb, bone in, about 6 pounds
Salt and freshly ground black pepper
2   tablespoons dried thyme or rosemary or a combination of the two
2   medium onions, peeled and chopped into large dice
2   medium carrots, cleaned and chopped into large dice

1. Preheat oven to 475°F.
2. Season lamb with salt and pepper to taste; sprinkle with herbs.
3. Place lamb on a rack in roasting pan and surround with chopped vegetables. Place in oven and roast 30 minutes, turning, to sear and brown all sides.
4. Turn down oven heat to 425°F and continue roasting until done, about 30 minutes.

Makes 8 portions

❧ ❧ ❧ Grilled Butterflied Leg of Lamb

Have the lamb boned and butterflied by your butcher. The long marination both tenderizes and flavors the meat.

1   boneless leg of lamb, butterflied, about 4–5 pounds
1   cup olive oil
Juice of 2 lemons
1   tablespoon minced fresh thyme
2   tablespoons minced fresh rosemary
2   tablespoons Dijon mustard
2   tablespoons salt
Freshly ground black pepper

1.   Place lamb in a shallow pan. Combine the rest of the ingredients to make a marinade. Pour over lamb. Marinate in refrigerator 24–48 hours.

2.   Prepare barbecue grill. When fire has burned down to embers, place lamb on grill and cook about 45 minutes. Turn every 10 minutes. Slice across the grain to serve.

Makes 6–8 portions

Variation: Lamb can also be broiled in a preheated broiler.

Leftover Lamb Patties with Yogurt and Parsley Sauce

Leg of lamb is reasonably priced, delicious, and easy to prepare. If the lamb is served rare, then the inevitable leftovers are very usable. These delicious patties make a wonderful luncheon dish. However, bear in mind that lamb has a high fat content.

2   pounds leftover cooked lamb
2   cloves garlic, peeled
Freshly ground black pepper
1   egg
½   tablespoon dried thyme
2   tablespoons olive oil
1½   cups Yogurt and Parsley Sauce (see Index)

1. Place lamb, garlic, pepper, egg, and thyme in a food processor fitted with a metal blade. Process in pulse mode until thoroughly blended.

2. Heat olive oil in a sauté pan. Form the lamb into eight patties and brown on both sides in the hot oil. Serve at once, accompanied by the yogurt sauce.

Makes 4 portions

❧ Marinated Flank Steak

Flank steak benefits from a hearty marinade such as this one. If you are broiling rather than grilling, make sure the broiler is very hot. Roasted Garlic (see Index) is a delicious accompaniment.

1   flank steak, about 3 pounds
1   tablespoon mustard
1   cup red wine
1   tablespoon whole black peppercorns
2   cloves garlic, peeled and mashed
Salt

1.   Place flank steak in a shallow pan. Combine mustard, wine, peppercorns, garlic, and salt to taste and pour over steak. Marinate in refrigerator 24-48 hours.

2.   Prepare a wood or charcoal fire and let it burn down to embers. Or preheat broiler. Remove steak from marinade and grill or broil 10-15 minutes, turning once. To serve, slice very thin on the diagonal.

Makes 4-6 portions

❧❧ Poached Fillet of Beef with Horseradish Sauce and Roasted Vegetables

This is a great dish for a spring or summer dinner because it can be served either hot or at room temperature. I have two pieces of advice: be careful not to overcook the beef fillet and be sure there are ample vegetables for each portion of meat. For ten diners, it is a good idea to triple the recipe for Roasted Vegetables and double the recipe for Horseradish Sauce (see Index).

1   whole fillet of beef, 3½–4½ pounds
Salt and freshly ground black pepper
2   quarts Brown Veal Stock (see Index)
Roasted Vegetables (triple recipe, see Index)
4   cups Horseradish Sauce (see Index)
Kitchen string for tying fillet

    1.   Tie string around each end of the fillet to help you remove it from pot later. Lightly salt and pepper fillet.

    2.   In a large pot, bring the veal stock to a simmer. Add the fillet and poach for 25 minutes.

    3.   While the fillet is poaching, prepare the Roasted Vegetables.

    4.   Remove finished meat from broth and place on a cutting board. At this point it will not look so great, but don't panic. Slice it into ten pieces and arrange on a long tray. Surround with Roasted Vegetables. Now it should look delicious. Serve Horseradish Sauce on the side.

Makes 10 portions

❧❧ Fillet Steak au Poivre

This is a delicious dish, and although it is not recommended for everyday eating, it certainly is too good to eliminate from your repertoire entirely. In my version, the steak is seared in a very hot pan, rather than sautéed in fat, as is traditional. You must use a heavy, cast-iron pan and preheat it 5 to 7 minutes.

Because the steaks are so sharply flavored, steamed vegetables make a good accompaniment.

¼   cup peppercorns
Salt
4   fillet steaks, about 1¼-1½ inches thick

1.   Preheat a heavy, cast-iron pan for 10 to 15 minutes, until very hot.

2.   Meanwhile, crush peppercorns: Put peppercorns on a cutting board. Lay the blade of a broad knife on top of them and pound your hand back and forth across the knife to crush the peppercorns coarsely. These will give the meat a pronounced pepper flavor.

3.   Lightly salt steaks. Coat both sides with peppercorns and press into steaks with your hands.

4.   Put steaks directly into pan and sear. Cook 3 minutes on each side for rare. Serve immediately.

Makes 4 portions

❧❧❧ Beef Stew with Winter Vegetables

I love this dish! Please be sure to brown the meat very well—most people do not brown meat thoroughly.

2	tablespoons oil
3	pounds beef (rump roast or chuck), cubed

Salt and freshly ground black pepper

3	medium carrots, scraped and coarsely sliced
1	medium onion, peeled and cut into eighths
4	medium parsnips, cut into rounds ⅛ inch thick
½	cup flour
3-4	cups Brown Veal Stock (see Index)
1	Bouquet Garni (see Index)
1	cup fresh or frozen peas

1. In a large, heavy pot, heat oil and brown meat very well. Sprinkle with salt and pepper. Remove meat from pot.

2. Add all vegetables except peas to pot and brown slightly, stirring often. Return meat to pot and sprinkle with flour. Cook 5-10 minutes to cook flour.

3. Add 1 cup stock and mix well to blend in flour. Add additional stock to cover meat. Add Bouquet Garni. Cover and simmer until meat is tender, about 1½ hours. Add peas for the last 2 minutes of cooking.

Makes 4 portions

Vegetables

Butternut Squash and Parsnip Puree

Carrot Puree

Grilled Carrots

Steamed Snow Peas and Carrots

Steamed Zucchini and Carrots

Batter-Fried Zucchini

Roasted Eggplant

Eggplant Puree

Braised Fennel

Steamed Haricots Verts

Parsley Steamed Potatoes

Steamed Spinach

Sautéed Cherry Tomatoes

Tomatoes Stuffed with Roasted Garlic and Shiitake Mushrooms

Mélange of Steamed Vegetables

Ratatouille

Puree of Turnips and Parsnips

Vegetables at their best provide a palette of colors, textures, and flavors any chef loves to work with. Many different vegetables were popular with our guests, from hearty spinach or peppers to elegant snow peas or haricots verts. Beautifully steamed fresh vegetables brighten up a plate and require no sauce and virtually no seasonings.

I preferred to steam vegetables whenever I could, once the Mayor decided to lighten his diet. I steamed them in a large pot with very little water on the bottom, as I explain in the section on steaming. Any vegetables can be done this way: snow peas, carrots, spinach, zucchini. Served without sauce and spiced with pepper only, they are as healthful as they are attractive.

Although roasted vegetables are not as pristinely healthful as steamed vegetables, they are perfectly acceptable. Only a small amount of oil is required in their preparation, and they are delicious. And they often provide a contrast in texture to the main course as, for instance, when served with poached fillet of beef.

Potatoes were often a favorite for formal dinners. But I rarely served them at small dinners or to the Mayor alone. The old theory of serving a starch with every main course is very much out of date. People prefer green and other colorful vegetables, and I usually served these with every meal.

❧ Butternut Squash and Parsnip Puree

  2 medium butternut squash, cut in halves, seeds removed
Water for steaming vegetables
  1 tablespoon butter
1-2 teaspoons grated fresh gingerroot (optional)
  2 medium parsnips, peeled, and cut into quarters
Salt and freshly ground black pepper

1. Preheat oven to 350°F.

2. Place squash halves cut side down in a baking pan and pour ½ inch water around squash. Bake 45 minutes or until tender.

3. Remove the squash flesh from the skin and puree in food processor with butter and ginger, if desired. Place in a bowl.

4. Meanwhile, steam parsnips 15 minutes or until tender. Puree in food processor and add to squash puree. Mix well. Season with salt and pepper to taste.

Makes 4 portions

❧ Carrot Puree

The final step in this recipe makes the result sublime. Reduce the cooking water to a rich glaze and use it to flavor the pureed vegetables.

1 bunch carrots, scrubbed and cut into ¼-inch rounds
Water to cover
1 tablespoon butter
Salt and freshly ground black pepper

1. Place carrots in pot and cover with water; add butter. Bring water to boil and cook carrots until tender. Drain.

2. Puree carrots in a food processor until smooth. Add salt and pepper to taste.

3. Boil cooking water until it is reduced to about 1 tablespoon, being careful not to burn. Combine this glaze with the puree.

Makes 4 portions

❧ Grilled Carrots

2   bunches fresh carrots cleaned and scraped, with ½ inch of green
       stems left on
Salt and freshly ground black pepper
2   tablespoons minced fresh thyme (*or* ½ tablespoon dried)

   1.   Prepare a charcoal fire and let it burn down to embers.
   2.   Place carrots on grill. Turn to brown each side. To avoid burning,
move them from the center of the grill to the sides as they brown. When
browned and somewhat limp, remove to serving platter. Sprinkle with salt
and pepper to taste and thyme. Serve immediately.

Makes 4 portions

Variation: For Grilled Onions, peel 2 onions, cut in half, and follow basic
recipe. For Grilled Mushrooms, clean 1 pound shiitake mushrooms,
remove stems, and follow basic recipe.

⚜ Steamed Snow Peas and Carrots

Before the Mayor's stroke in 1987, I would have sautéed these vegetables. I found steaming to be a good alternative to sautéing—in fact, I prefer vegetables prepared this lighter, more healthful way.

2 medium carrots, peeled
½ pound snow peas, tops cut off and strings removed
Water for steaming
Salt and freshly ground black pepper

1. Cut carrots into julienne. Cut snow peas on an angle into ½-inch lengths.
2. Bring ½ inch water to boil in a large pot. Add carrots, cover, and steam for 30 seconds. Add snow peas, cover, and steam for an additional 20 seconds.
3. Drain vegetables and add salt and pepper to taste. Serve at once.

Makes 4 portions

⚜ Steamed Zucchini and Carrots

This goes beautifully with almost any dish, but bear in mind that the flavor is very delicate.

1 medium zucchini, scrubbed and ends trimmed
2 medium carrots, scraped and ends trimmed
Water for steaming
Salt and freshly ground black pepper

1. Cut zucchini and carrots into 2-inch pieces and cut those pieces into rectangles and then into julienne.
2. Steam carrots 30 seconds in a steamer or in a small amount of boiling water. Add zucchini and steam another 20 seconds. Season with salt and pepper to taste and serve immediately.

Makes 4 portions

Variation: During the summer, cherry tomatoes are excellent cut in halves and added to this dish. No need to cook the tomatoes; just toss with the carrots and zucchini.

✿✿✿ Batter-Fried Zucchini

Although this recipe is not slimming, it is light in feeling because the batter does not overwhelm the vegetables. I prepared it only rarely, but whenever it appeared on the Mayor's table, it brought a smile.

1 large egg lightly beaten, plus water to equal 1 cup in all
¾ cup flour
Safflower oil for frying
3 medium zucchini
Juice of ½ lemon
Salt

1. Combine eggs, water, and flour to form a light batter.

2. Pour oil into frying pan to a depth of 2 inches and heat until very hot.

3. Cut zucchini into julienne. Dip into batter and fry in hot oil until golden brown.

4. Drain zucchini on paper towels. Sprinkle with lemon juice and salt to taste. Serve at once.

Makes 4 portions

❧ Roasted Eggplant

Accompanied by Light Tomato Sauce (see Index), this is delicious with grilled meats, fish, and chicken.

You can also make this dish with white eggplants. They are slightly less acidic than the purple and equally flavorful.

2 medium eggplants, split lengthwise
Salt and freshly ground black pepper
2 tablespoons olive oil
4 cloves garlic, peeled and cut into slivers
Basil for garnish

1. Preheat oven to 400°F.

2. Score eggplant flesh horizontally and vertically with a knife point. Sprinkle with salt and pepper to taste. Drizzle with olive oil. Insert garlic slivers into flesh. Place in a lightly oiled baking dish skin side down and bake until top is browned, 20-25 minutes. Garnish each serving with a sprig of basil.

Makes 4 portions

❧ Eggplant Puree

This puree can be served warm or cold.

2   medium eggplants, split lengthwise
2   tablespoons olive oil
Salt and freshly ground black pepper

1.   Preheat oven to 400°F.
2.   Rub a baking pan with olive oil. Score the cut side of the eggplant and brush with olive oil. Sprinkle lightly with salt and pepper. Place in pan skin side down.
3.   Roast 20–25 minutes.
4.   Remove from oven. Scoop out flesh and place in container of food processor. In the pulse mode, process to a rough puree.

Makes 4 portions

Variation: While eggplant is roasting, add to pan 6 cloves garlic, unpeeled, slightly mashed. After roasting, peel garlic and puree along with eggplant.

❧ Braised Fennel

This is an excellent way to prepare fennel, a vegetable with the definite flavor of anise. First sauté the fennel in a combination of olive oil and butter. I leave the proportions up to you—all you actually need is a hint of butter for flavor. Then braise the vegetable in the oven until done.

4   teaspoons olive oil and butter combined
1   medium bulb fennel or two small bulbs, with 1 inch of stem left
        on so that bulb stays together
Salt and freshly ground black pepper
½   cup Chicken Stock (see Index)
Water as needed
½   cup grated Parmesan

1.   Preheat oven to 450°F.

2.   Heat oil and butter in a sauté pan large enough to accommodate fennel. Sauté fennel until slightly brown. Season with salt and pepper.

3.   Add Chicken Stock to pan. Place in oven for 15 minutes, adding water if stock evaporates.

4.   Sprinkle with grated cheese and cook 5 minutes more. Keep warm until served.

Makes 4 portions

❧ Steamed Haricots Verts

These beans go wonderfully well with lamb, fish, chicken, and veal and add a bit of elegance to the plate.

Water
¾-1 pound haricots verts, washed and tips cut off
Salt and freshly ground black pepper

1. Put ½ inch water in a large pot and bring to boil. Add beans, cover, and cook beans 8–10 minutes. Remove from pot.
2. If beans are to be served hot, season with salt and pepper to taste and serve immediately. If beans will be used in a salad, plunge them into a bowl of ice water. Remove and dry and proceed with salad recipe.

Makes 4 portions

❧ Parsley Steamed Potatoes

These delicate steamed potatoes are excellent with or without the optional butter. The amount of butter called for is very small, just enough to enhance the flavor of the potatoes.

Water for steaming
1 pound new potatoes, washed and cut in halves
2 tablespoons chopped parsley
Salt and freshly ground black pepper
1 tablespoon butter (optional)

1. Place a small amount of water in a large pot and bring to a boil. Steam potatoes (or cook directly in the water) until cooked but still firm. Do not overcook.
2. Put potatoes in a bowl and toss with parsley, salt and pepper to taste, and butter, if desired. Serve at once.

Makes 4 portions

❧   Steamed Spinach

Spinach prepared this way is excellent. Since it is barely cooked, it retains all its natural, fresh flavor.

1   pound fresh spinach
Freshly ground black pepper

1.   Remove stems from spinach. Wash leaves well.
2.   Place leaves, with water still clinging to them, in 10-inch frying pan. Season with freshly ground black pepper to taste. Cover pan.
3.   Place pan over high heat and shake 1½ minutes. Remove from heat and serve immediately.

Makes 4 portions

❧   Sautéed Cherry Tomatoes

This simple dish is an excellent accompaniment to Sautéed Chicken with Pesto (see Index), since tomatoes go so well with the basil and garlic in the sauce. It also looks and tastes great with grilled fish or chicken.

1   tablespoon olive oil
1   pound ripe cherry tomatoes, washed and stems removed
Salt and freshly ground black pepper

Heat olive oil in a frying pan. Gently sauté cherry tomatoes just to warm through. The skin should not break. Sprinkle with salt and pepper to taste and serve immediately.

Makes 4 portions

❧ Tomatoes Stuffed with Roasted Garlic and Shiitake Mushrooms

These tomatoes are delicious served with Roast Leg of Lamb (see Index). The roasted garlic has a mild flavor, which sets off the richly flavored mushrooms and the slightly acidic tomatoes.

2   heads garlic
4   ripe tomatoes (from a local farm if possible)
½   tablespoon olive oil
¼   pound shiitake mushrooms, stems removed and caps cut into
        julienne
Freshly ground black pepper

1.   Preheat oven to 350°F. Make Roasted Garlic (see Index).

2.   Slice tops off tomatoes about ¼ inch down and scrape out tomato seeds and pulp. Reserve tops.

3.   Heat oil in frying pan and sauté mushrooms.

4.   When garlic is done, peel cloves and toss with mushrooms. Stuff tomatoes with mixture and replace their tops.

5.   Return to oven approximately 10 minutes. Remove, season with pepper to taste, and serve immediately.

Makes 4 portions

❦❦ Mélange of Steamed Vegetables

This is a beautiful treat: a bright combination of broccoli, cauliflower, and zucchini, steamed until crisp-tender and made sprightly by the addition of cherry tomatoes and fresh herbs. Without the optional Pesto Sauce this dish is rated light.

Water for steaming
1   head broccoli, washed, florets only
1   head cauliflower, washed and cut into florets
1   medium zucchini, scrubbed and cut into ¼-inch rounds
1   dozen cherry tomatoes, rinsed and cut into halves
1   tablespoon fresh thyme, tarragon, and oregano, mixed
¼   cup Basil Vinaigrette or Light Pesto Sauce (optional, see Index)

1.   Place about ½ inch water in a heavy pot. Bring to boil and add broccoli and cauliflower. Steam 1 minute. Add zucchini. Steam 30 seconds. Remove from pot.

2.   Combine with cherry tomatoes.

3.   Sprinkle with fresh herbs and toss with vinaigrette or pesto sauce, if desired.

Makes 4 portions

✿ Ratatouille

Don't cut all these vegetables into miniature pieces; cut them into rather large dice, and they will look much more attractive and retain their texture through cooking.

This dish should be done quickly and effortlessly. You don't have to measure out all your ingredients—be creative. And you don't have to cook the vegetables for hours. I much prefer a ratatouille that has been only briefly cooked to one that has been cooked to death.

2   medium onions, peeled
4   red peppers
2   medium zucchini
1   medium eggplant, peeled
3   tablespoons olive oil
6   cloves garlic, peeled and crushed
1   28-ounce can whole tomatoes, drained and crushed
Salt and freshly ground black pepper

1.   Cut the onions, peppers, zucchini, and eggplant into large dice.

2.   Heat 2 tablespoons of the olive oil in a large pan and sauté onion, peppers, and zucchini for 3 minutes. Remove to a bowl.

3.   Heat the remaining 1 tablespoon olive oil and sauté eggplant 3 minutes. Remove to bowl.

4.   Add garlic to pan and cook 30 seconds. Add tomatoes and cook 2 minutes.

5.   Return all vegetables to pan and simmer 20 minutes. Season with salt and pepper to taste.

Makes 4-6 portions

❧ Puree of Turnips and Parsnips

This is a classic vegetable accompaniment to the Thanksgiving turkey. A small amount of butter enriches the puree. If you want an extra hint of sweetness, add a teaspoonful of sugar.

2   medium parsnips, scraped and cut into medium dice
1   medium turnip, peeled and cut into medium dice
Water to cover vegetables
1   tablespoon butter
1   teaspoon sugar (optional)
Salt and freshly ground black pepper

1.   Place vegetables in pot and cover with water. Add butter and sugar, if desired. Bring water to a simmer and cook vegetables until tender. Drain. Reserve cooking water.

2.   Place vegetables in food processor and puree, using the pulse mode. Add salt and pepper to taste.

3.   Boil the cooking water until it is reduced to 1 tablespoon. Combine this glaze with the puree.

Makes 4 portions

Salads

Arugula and Roasted Red Pepper Salad

Arugula with Balsamic Vinaigrette

Tomato and Arugula Salad with Marinated Mussels

Bibb Lettuce, Goat Cheese, and Red Pepper Salad

Fennel with Bibb Lettuce

Endive and Watercress Salad

Tomato Salad

Artichoke Hearts and Lobster with Raspberry Vinaigrette

Haricots Verts Salad

Cucumber, Tomato, and Onion Salad

Caesar Salad

In a way, I owe my career as a chef to salads. When I was in boarding school in Israel I worked in the garden growing the most beautiful romaine lettuce imaginable. I couldn't resist the temptation to pick some of that romaine for myself. I crept down to the garden late at night and did just that. Hiding in my room, I whipped up a vinaigrette with ingredients charitably offered me by the cook. The result was magnificent, as only fresh-picked salad can be. It was clear to me that the food I prepared was far better than anything I was served by others. I decided then and there to become a professional chef.

I am still inspired by salads, and I served a lot of them at Gracie Mansion. A beautiful fresh salad was always welcome at lunch or at dinner. I served the salad course before the main course, and whichever salad I chose, I included plenty of garlic for the Mayor.

I have already stated that Caesar Salad is among my favorite dishes—one of the treats I prepare when I am cooking for myself alone. Another favorite of mine—and of the Mayor's—was Arugula with Balsamic Vinaigrette.

The easiest salads to make are combinations of fresh greens dressed with any interesting vinaigrette. You can't fail with a simple salad of arugula or Fennel with Bibb Lettuce or Endive and Watercress. But slightly more elaborate salads are delicious, too. Try the Bibb Lettuce, Goat Cheese, and Red Pepper with Orange Vinaigrette or the salad of Artichoke Hearts and Lobster with Raspberry Vinaigrette, which is a festive meal in itself.

A word about nutritional rating: you may be surprised that these salads are rated "rich." The reason is that the vinaigrettes, while lighter than classic dressings, contain oil in excess of our "light" guidelines. However, the amount of dressing you use is up to you, so you can lighten these salads by cutting down on the dressings. If you substitute either of the light dressings (Extra-Light Dressing or Yogurt and Garlic Dressing) for a vinaigrette, you will lighten them even more.

❧❧❧ Arugula and Roasted Red Pepper Salad

Arugula is very delicate, so treat it gently. Remove stems with your hands, not a knife. Wash it carefully, twice, to remove grit.

3 Roasted Peppers (see Index)
3 bunches arugula, well washed
4 tablespoons olive oil
¼ cup balsamic vinegar
Freshly ground black pepper

1.   Cut peppers into julienne and place in salad bowl. Tear arugula and place in salad bowl.
2.   Combine oil and vinegar and pour over peppers and arugula. Season with pepper to taste. Toss and serve at once.

Makes 4 portions

❧❧❧ Arugula with Balsamic Vinaigrette

3 ripe tomatoes
3 bunches arugula
Freshly ground black pepper
½ cup Balsamic Vinaigrette (see Index)

Slice tomatoes very, very thin. For each serving, arrange tomatoes on a plate in concentric circles. Break up arugula with your hands and mound on top of tomatoes. Season with pepper to taste and drizzle with Balsamic Vinaigrette.

Makes 4 portions

❧❧❧ Tomato and Arugula Salad with Marinated Mussels

Be sure to choose the small mussels for this salad; they are sweeter and more tender than the large. Out of the 3–4 dozen you steam, some will not open and will have to be discarded.

Although I give ingredients to make about 1 cup of vinaigrette, you will probably use less than half that amount. First of all, the mussels are marinated in the vinaigrette and then removed from it. When you serve the salad, you can use as little of the dressing as you choose. You can lighten this salad to your individual taste.

1	cup dry white wine
Pinch dried thyme	
3	sprigs parsley
½	medium onion, chopped fine
3–4	dozen small mussels, cleaned
1	tablespoon mustard
¼	cup tarragon vinegar
¾	cup olive oil
Freshly ground black pepper	
3	bunches arugula, well washed
2	large tomatoes

1. Combine wine, thyme, parsley, and onion in a medium pot and bring to boil. Add mussels, cover, and let steam 1–2 minutes. Remove mussels and discard any that have not opened.

2. Whisk together mustard, vinegar, olive oil, and pepper to taste. Remove mussels from shells and marinate in mixture 20 minutes at room temperature.

3. Remove stems from arugula. Cut tomatoes into ¼-inch dice and toss with arugula. Add mussels and as much or as little of the dressing (marinade) as you prefer and toss again. Serve at room temperature.

Makes 4 portions

❧❧❧ Bibb Lettuce, Goat Cheese, and Red Pepper Salad

Goat cheese and red pepper are a perfect combination, and this salad can be the main course for a summer luncheon. The goat cheese takes it out of the light category, however.

3   heads Bibb lettuce, washed and dried
4   Roasted Peppers (see Index)
1   log (about ½ pound) creamy goat cheese
Freshly ground black pepper
¾   cup Orange Vinaigrette (see Index)

1.   Combine lettuce and red peppers and toss. Crumble cheese and add to salad. Season with pepper to taste.

2.   Add dressing to taste and toss again.

Makes 4 portions

Variation: Substitute Basil Vinaigrette (see Index) for the Orange Vinaigrette. Add a few cloves of peeled Roasted Garlic (see Index) to each serving of salad.

❧❧❧ Fennel with Bibb Lettuce

Fennel adds a wonderful fresh taste and a hint of anise to this salad.

1   bulb fennel
2   heads Bibb lettuce
1   pint cherry tomatoes, cut into halves
½   cup Basic Vinaigrette with Fresh Herbs (see Index)

1.   Wash fennel bulb and cut into julienne. Wash and dry lettuce. Combine greens and cherry tomatoes.

2.   Add dressing to taste.

Makes 4 portions

❧❧❧   Endive and Watercress Salad

2   heads endive
1   bunch watercress
1   pint cherry tomatoes, cut into halves
Freshly ground black pepper
½   cup Basic Vinaigrette with Fresh Herbs (see Index)

1.   Wash and dry endive. Cut off bottoms of each head and separate leaves. Cut leaves into julienne.

2.   Wash and dry watercress; remove stems.

3.   Combine endive and watercress and mound on individual plates. Garnish with halved cherry tomatoes. Season with fresh pepper to taste. Drizzle with vinaigrette.

Makes 4 portions

❧❧❧   Tomato Salad

I have never understood why in the summer months it is so difficult to get a delicious tomato salad in many restaurants. The key to a perfect salad is obviously the tomatoes (not that you needed this book to tell you that). To me, local tomatoes are the best for just slicing and eating, and the less you do to them, the better. Since I live in New York, I am lucky enough to have access to the excellent New Jersey tomatoes.

Tomatoes are at their best in July and August, and that is the only time tomato salad appears on my table.

4   medium beefsteak tomatoes
½   cup Basil Vinaigrette (see Index)
1   bunch fresh basil

1.   Cut tomatoes in half; core; cut in half again. Cut 4 wedges from each section.

2.   Arrange wedges on four plates in a fan shape around edge of plate. Make a second fan on the plate's interior, reversing the points of the wedges. Cover lightly with vinaigrette and basil leaves.

Makes 4 portions

❧❧❧ Artichoke Hearts and Lobster with Raspberry Vinaigrette

This is a beautiful presentation for a summer dinner or lunch, with the green vegetables highlighting the white shellfish. The preparation is somewhat complicated, but well worth the effort.

The best dessert for this main course—from both the nutritional and the aesthetic points of view—is ripe, delicious, fresh fruit.

4   artichokes
1   quart water for artichokes plus enough water to cover lobsters
Few teaspoons salt
Juice of ½ lemon
½   recipe Haricots Verts Salad (see Index)
4   live lobsters, 2 pounds each
1   tablespoon Dijon mustard
2   tablespoons raspberry vinegar
1   sprig fresh or pinch dried tarragon
6   tablespoons olive oil
Fresh coriander (cilantro) leaves for garnish

1.   Using a stainless steel knife so as not to discolor the artichokes, remove outer leaves and cut out hearts. Discard leaves.

2.   Bring water to boil in medium-size pot and add pinch salt and lemon juice. Simmer artichoke hearts approximately 30 minutes or until tender. Remove and let cool.

3.   Divide Haricots Verts Salad among 4 artichoke hearts, mounding about 1 inch high on each heart.

4.   Prepare lobsters: Fill large pot with enough water to cover lobsters. Add 1 teaspoon salt per quart of water and bring to a boil. Plunge lobsters head first into the rapidly boiling salted water. Boil 15–20 minutes.

5.   Remove lobsters and split in half without cutting the tails. Remove tail meat from each lobster in one piece.

6.   Prepare vinaigrette: Mix mustard, vinegar, and tarragon. Slowly add olive oil, whisking mixture until it thickens.

7.   To serve, slice tail meat into thin slices and arrange around the perimeter of four plates. Place a stuffed artichoke heart in the center of each plate and top with meat from lobster claws. Run a circle of vinaigrette around the artichoke heart so that it just touches the tips of the lobster slices. Sprinkle lobster with whole coriander leaves.

Makes 4 portions

184

❧❧ Haricots Verts Salad

2 quarts water
½ pound green beans, washed and tips cut off
Bowl of ice water
About 2 tablespoons Pesto (see Index)
Salt and freshly ground black pepper

1. In a large pot, bring water to boil.
2. Add beans and cook until bright green, about 2 minutes.
3. Remove beans and plunge into ice water.
4. Drain and cut into ⅛-inch pieces.
5. Blend with Pesto sauce. Salt and pepper to taste.

Makes 4 portions

❧❧ Cucumber, Tomato, and Onion Salad

What makes this salad so good is its simplicity. It is a delicious accompaniment to almost any main dish.

2 firm medium cucumbers
2 ripe medium tomatoes
1 medium Spanish onion
4 tablespoons olive oil
Juice of 1 lemon
1 tablespoon vinegar
Salt and freshly ground black pepper

1. Peel and seed cucumbers. Peel tomatoes and onion. Cut all vegetables into medium dice.

2. Place vegetables in a salad bowl. Combine olive oil, lemon juice, and vinegar and pour over vegetables. Mix well and season to taste with salt and pepper.

Makes 4 portions

⚜⚜⚜ Caesar Salad

I often made this salad for Mayor Koch when he came home late at night and did not want a full dinner. It is easy to prepare on the spur of the moment, yet it is special and satisfying. Though not light by our nutritional standards, it most certainly is not the kind of meal that will weigh you down.

1   egg yolk
1   tablespoon Dijon mustard
4   fillets of anchovies, rinsed to remove excess salt, if desired
2-3   cloves garlic, peeled
¼   cup olive oil
Juice of 1 lemon
6   tablespoons grated Parmesan
Freshly ground black pepper
1   head romaine lettuce, large outside leaves removed, remaining leaves washed and dried and broken into bite-sized pieces

1.   Place egg yolk, mustard, anchovies, and garlic in a large wooden salad bowl. Using a fork, mash garlic and anchovies together and blend with yolk and mustard. Add oil slowly, mixing continually with fork. Add lemon juice, half the cheese, and pepper to taste, mixing until dressing thickens.

2.   Just before serving, add lettuce and remaining cheese to bowl and toss with dressing.

Makes 2 portions

Salad Dressings

Basic Vinaigrette with Fresh Herbs

Chervil Vinaigrette

Orange Vinaigrette

Basil Vinaigrette

Balsamic Vinaigrette

Extra-Light Dressing (Vinegar, Lemon, and Mustard)

Yogurt and Garlic Dressing

When you serve salads several nights a week, as I did at Gracie Mansion, it is a good idea to have a variety of vinaigrettes in your repertoire. Use pure virgin olive oil and a good quality vinegar. I give several vinaigrettes, as well as two totally oil-free dressings, the Extra-Light and the Yogurt and Garlic dressings.

All but the last two dressings are rated "rich." This is because, even though they are lighter than classical vinaigrettes, they still contain enough oil to move them out of the "light" category.

When you make a vinaigrette, put the mustard and vinegar in the bowl first and add oil slowly, stirring with a fork. The only tools you need are a small bowl and a fork—don't invest in anything expensive. Don't bother with a jar and lid, either. I think a vinaigrette that is shaken in a jar is not as good as one mixed in a bowl.

❧❧❧ Basic Vinaigrette with Fresh Herbs

6   tablespoons olive oil
2   tablespoons white wine vinegar
1   tablespoon Dijon mustard
2   cloves garlic, peeled and mashed
1   tablespoon each minced fresh thyme, tarragon, chives, and parsley
Freshly ground black pepper

Place ingredients in a small bowl and combine with a fork.

Makes ¾ cup

❧❧❧ Chervil Vinaigrette

Chervil is a delicate herb that resembles parsley in appearance. It is not used often enough.

Use a delicate white wine vinegar—a strongly flavored vinegar will overwhelm the herb.

6   tablespoons olive oil
2   tablespoons white wine vinegar
1   tablespoon Dijon mustard
3   tablespoons fresh chervil, minced
Freshly ground black pepper

Place all ingredients in a small bowl and combine with a fork. This dressing is delicious on Bibb, red leaf, or Boston lettuce. It is excellent on mâche, also known as lamb's lettuce, because this delicate salad green has a very subtle flavor that goes well with chervil.

Makes ¾ cup

⚜⚜⚜ Orange Vinaigrette

When you grate the orange rind for this vinaigrette, be sure to use only the orange outer skin because the white part, or pith, is bitter.

In addition to serving this dressing on salads, try it on cold steamed asparagus.

6   tablespoons olive oil
2   tablespoons white wine vinegar
1   tablespoon Dijon mustard
Grated rind of 1 medium orange
1   tablespoon minced fresh thyme
Freshly ground black pepper

Place all ingredients in a small bowl and combine with a fork. Serve over Bibb, red leaf, or Boston lettuce.

Makes ¾ cup

⚜⚜⚜ Balsamic Vinaigrette

6   tablespoons olive oil
2   tablespoons balsamic vinegar
1   tablespoon Dijon mustard
1   clove garlic, peeled and mashed
Freshly ground black pepper

Place ingredients in a small bowl and combine with a fork.

Makes ½ cup

❧❧❧ Basil Vinaigrette

Depending upon what you plan to serve this dressing with, you can increase the garlic or even omit it altogether. This is an excellent dressing for tomatoes.

6   tablespoons olive oil
2   tablespoons white wine vinegar
1   tablespoon Dijon mustard
1-2   cloves garlic, peeled and crushed
Freshly ground black pepper
½   cup fresh basil leaves, julienned

Place all ingredients except basil in small bowl and combine with a fork. Add basil to the dressing just before serving.

Makes ¾ cup

❧ Extra-Light Dressing (Vinegar, Lemon, and Mustard)

This light dressing is especially tangy. If it is somewhat sharp for your taste, add a small amount of water.

2   tablespoons white wine vinegar
1   tablespoon lemon juice
1   tablespoon Dijon mustard
½   tablespoon water
1   clove garlic, peeled and crushed
Freshly ground black pepper

Place all ingredients in a small bowl and blend with a fork.

Makes ¼ cup

❧ Yogurt and Garlic Dressing

You will find that this dressing has a wonderful richness, but it is rated "light" because it contains no oil.

1   cup plain low-fat or nonfat yogurt
1   tablespoon lemon juice
2   cloves garlic, peeled and crushed
2   tablespoons chopped parsley
Freshly ground black pepper

Place all ingredients in a small bowl and combine with a fork.

Makes 1 cup

Desserts

Grapefruit Sorbet

Poached Pears with Two Fruit Purees

Marinated Fruit

Strawberries with Raspberry Puree

Elaine London's Home-Canned Peaches

Gogol-Mogol

On a beautiful, balmy July evening, Mayor Koch invited several close personal friends for dinner. Anticipating that the weather and the company would be most pleasant, I went all out in planning a rainbow of summer desserts—six in all. In addition to a caloric chocolate treat for the diehards and a sublime tarte tatin, I offered the following: white peaches from California, tiny, sweet New York State strawberries, and dewy, delicious New Jersey blueberries. As a kind of middle ground, I created perfect miniature tarts from the strawberries and blueberries. Every guest but one requested fresh fruit—not because the party was particularly health-conscious, but because the peaches and berries, in the height of their season, were simply irresistible. Several asked to taste the more caloric desserts as well, I must admit, but this does not in any way lessen the appeal of that glorious fruit.

These particular guests had eaten my meals for about seven years, and they knew what to expect. I always offered the freshest fruit as well as fresh fruit juices at Gracie Mansion. Sadly, it is often easier to get good cake in New York City restaurants than good fruit. Many restaurants do not make the effort to present fresh desserts as appealing as mine. But you can serve the best at home. Here are my pointers for selecting fruit:

First and most important, choose each variety of fruit in its season. The strawberries you buy in winter and the grapefruit you buy in August will be expensive and of lesser quality.

Second, find a reliable produce person. He will help you in selections and will even take back that box of peaches that promised perfection and lied.

Here is some information on individual fruits, berries, and melons.

PEACHES

Choose peaches by smell and color. They should smell sweet and "peachy" and be orange-yellow. Never buy green peaches—they won't ripen properly at home. Ripe peaches should not be too firm. If you buy firm (but not green) peaches, you can ripen them at room temperature. Peaches are very tricky and even after passing the smell and color test may sometimes turn out mealy or mushy if they are even a little past the height of their season. That is where your reliable produce person comes in. You can buy good peaches all summer long and into the fall.

PEARS

Bartlett pears are best from August through October. They can be yellow or red when ripe and should be large and firm—never mushy. Green Anjou and brown bosc pears are best from October through May. They should be firm but not hard.

STRAWBERRIES

Choose strawberries from April through August by smell, appearance, and taste. They should be red and shiny with green caps and stems. The distinct smell of a perfect strawberry is unmistakable. While I was at Gracie Mansion, I was lucky enough to get strawberries from Long Island and upstate New York, which are superb.

RASPBERRIES

Raspberries are in season in July, August, and September. Look for a dark reddish color and a mild scent. Taste is ultimately the best test for raspberries.

BLUEBERRIES

You can buy blueberries from May until late August. They should be purplish blue and have a powdery appearance. They should not appear dried out or mushy.

BING CHERRIES

A deep, dark red-brown color, shiny skin, and firmness to the touch indicate ripeness. Cherries are in season during June, July, and August.

WHITE CHERRIES

This exotic fruit has a very short season. If you find a good batch when they are at their best, in May, buy a case, because tomorrow may be too late. They should be creamy yellow and reddish in color and firm to the touch. Taste one before buying.

CANTALOUPE AND HONEYDEW

Choose heavy melons that are not green. Cantaloupes should smell sweet and melony. The stem end should be slightly soft when you press it. Buy in July through September.

TEMPLE ORANGES

Available December through May, these oranges are great for juice and simply the best in flavor.

As perfect as fresh fruit can be, there are times you may want something a little different. For a variation try the Grapefruit or Orange Sorbet or the Strawberries with Raspberry Puree. They are wonderfully simple to prepare and are light and delicious. And treat yourself to the Poached Pears with Two Fruit Purees, the marinated fruits, and my mother's extraordinary home-canned peaches. (These last three don't receive a "light" rating because of their sugar content.)

I also include a citrus-rich drink, even though it is not a dessert, because it is fruit based. It is a combination cold remedy and treat.

❧ Grapefruit Sorbet

1   cup sugar
2   cups water
3   cups freshly squeezed grapefruit juice
1   tablespoon grated grapefruit rind

1.   Combine sugar and water in saucepan and bring to boil. Simmer 5 minutes, remove from heat, and let cool.

2.   Combine cooled syrup, juice, and rind and refrigerate. When chilled, freeze in an ice-cream maker according to manufacturer's directions.

Makes 1 quart

Variation: For Orange Sorbet, substitute fresh orange juice and orange rind for the grapefruit juice and rind.

❧❧ Poached Pears with Two Fruit Purees

Poached Pears
- 4 cups water
- 1 cup sugar
- 1 stick cinnamon
- 2 cloves
- 4 bosc pears with stems

Purees
- 1 medium mango, peeled and cubed
- 3½–4 tablespoons sugar
- 1 pint fresh raspberries (*or* 1 10-ounce box frozen)

Few drops fresh lemon juice

1. Combine water, 1 cup sugar, cinnamon, and cloves in a large pot and bring to a boil. Simmer 20 minutes.

2. Peel pears and cut a very small amount off bottoms so they can stand up. Add pears to pot with syrup and simmer 15–20 minutes.

3. Place mango chunks and ½–1 tablespoon sugar (depending upon ripeness of fruit) in a food processor fitted with a steel blade. Puree fruit and set aside.

4. Place fresh raspberries and 3 tablespoons sugar in processor or use frozen raspberries with no additional sugar. Puree berries. Remove puree from processor, strain, mix in lemon juice, and set aside.

5. On each of four dessert plates, stand 1 poached pear. Spoon some mango puree on one side of pear and some raspberry puree on the other side.

Makes 4 portions

❧❧ Marinated Fruit

This is a beautiful and impressive dessert, suitable for your most elegant dinner party.

Syrup
2½ cups sugar
2 cups water
1 tablespoon Calvados

Fruit
Water to cover fruit
2 grapefruit
2 navel oranges
2 bosc pears
1 pint raspberries
Fresh mint leaves for garnish

1. Combine sugar and water in a large pot and bring to a boil. Boil 4–5 minutes. Remove from heat and let cool 30 minutes. Add Calvados.

2. Bring enough water to cover oranges and grapefruit to a boil and drop oranges and grapefruit into it for 10 seconds. This will make peeling them easier.

3. Holding each orange and grapefruit over a bowl to catch the juice, peel with a very sharp knife. Remove all the outer skin and white pith. Cut each section completely away from the membrane.

4. Peel and seed pears and cut each into 6–8 wedges.

5. Add all fruit and juices to syrup and marinate 4–6 hours.

6. Arrange marinated fruit on four dessert plates or a large serving platter. Scatter raspberries over all and garnish with mint leaves.

Makes 4 portions

❧ Strawberries with Raspberry Puree

Prepare this simple dessert only when strawberries are in season, from April through August. Pick the freshest, sweetest-smelling local berries you can find.

1 pint raspberries (*or* 1 10-ounce box frozen raspberries)
3 tablespoons sugar
Few drops fresh lemon juice
1 quart strawberries

1. Place raspberries and sugar in a food processor fitted with a steel blade. If you are using frozen raspberries, thaw slightly and place in processor with no additional sugar. Puree raspberries. Remove from processor, strain, and mix in lemon juice.

2. Wash strawberries and remove stems. Divide berries among four dessert plates and spoon the raspberry puree around the berries.

Makes 4 portions

❧❧❧ Elaine London's Home-Canned Peaches

My mother usually cans these peaches in huge quantities, but here I give the recipe for 4 quarts. You need about 1 cup syrup per quart of fruit, so you can increase the recipe if you choose. The syrup allowance is generous, because as the peaches cook, they release juice into the syrup and increase its volume. So you may have some delicious leftover peach syrup after you have finished canning.

My mother insists upon beautiful, firm, ripe peaches. She especially likes those with red centers, because they produce a lovely pink-tinted syrup.

We consider this recipe rich because of the sugar content.

Peaches
4 quarts firm, ripe peaches, bought at the height of the season
Boiling water for blanching

Light Syrup
1¼ cups sugar
4 cups water

1. Sterilize four 1-quart canning jars and lids according to manufacturer's directions.

2. Blanch peaches in a large pot of boiling water for 10 seconds. Remove from water, peel, cut in halves, remove pits, and cut away any blemishes.

3. Prepare syrup: boil sugar and water 5 minutes, skimming foam from the top.

4. Add peaches to syrup and simmer 4–8 minutes until tender but firm. They should not be soft.

5. Pack hot fruit in overlapping layers into hot jars, to within 1 inch of top of each jar. Pour 1 cup syrup over each quart of packed fruit, coming right up to the top of the jar. Fill and seal jars one at a time—not assembly-line fashion.

Makes 4 quarts

❧ Gogol-Mogol

This is not a dessert—it is a hot citrus drink that is good for what ails you. When I came to work at Gracie Mansion, the Mayor described it to me (I had never heard of it before). He often asked me to give the recipe to someone suffering from a cold.

I understand the original Russian drink was made with milk, eggs, and honey and was prescribed as a remedy for winter colds and flu.

2 oranges
1 grapefruit
1 lemon
1 lime
1 teaspoon honey
Splash of Cognac

Squeeze fruit and place juices in a small pot. Heat just to boiling point. Place honey and Cognac in a mug and add hot juices. Drink at once.

Makes 1 portion

Thanksgiving

Roast Turkey with Gravy

Stuffing

Cranberry-Orange Relish

Puree of Carrots with Ginger

Candied Sweet Potatoes

Steamed Green Beans

Applesauce

Mayor Koch's Thanksgiving celebration at Gracie Mansion was one of my favorite events. It was great fun to cook for such a festive occasion and to prepare classic American dishes.

Because I knew what the Mayor's guests preferred, my menu varied little, if at all, from year to year. I prepared a traditional Thanksgiving dinner and, I must admit, did not lighten the dishes. You may feel some of these recipes are out of place in a cookbook that tries to stress lightness. But remember that Thanksgiving, after all, is a day that celebrates the blessings of bountiful food and good company.

Throughout my years at Gracie Mansion, Mayor Koch began his Thanksgiving day the same way: he arose early and distributed the eight hundred to one thousand cookies I had baked to people at shelters, prisons, and firehouses all over the city. He followed this same routine every Christmas morning, as well. Dinner began about three or four in the afternoon, and proceeded at a relaxed pace.

Here is the menu for Thanksgiving dinner, which I repeated for seven consecutive years. Recipes that appear elsewhere in this book are marked with an asterisk; new recipes follow the menu. These new recipes all serve twelve diners. You can triple the other recipes for a party of that number. I would suggest that you make extra portions of the Mushroom Soup—I served a lot of seconds. I don't include a dessert in this menu, because the Mayor's guests usually brought something sweet.

Mushroom Soup*
Roast Turkey with Gravy
Stuffing
Cranberry-Orange Relish
Candied Sweet Potatoes
Puree of Carrots with Ginger
Puree of Turnips and Parsnips*
Steamed Green Beans
Roasted Shiitake Mushrooms*
Applesauce

---

*See Index for recipes.

❧❧ Roast Turkey with Gravy

This is the traditional centerpiece of a Thanksgiving feast, prepared as simply as possible. I cooked the stuffing separately, which I think ensures the best results.

Turkey
1   turkey, about 18 pounds
Salt and freshly ground black pepper
½   cup butter, melted
Kitchen string for tying the legs

Gravy
4   cups Chicken Stock (see Index)
3   tablespoons flour

1.   Preheat oven to 450°F.

2.   Season turkey inside and out with salt and pepper to taste. Tie legs together. Place breast side up on a rack in a roasting pan and roast uncovered until tender, about 4½ hours or 15 minutes per pound. After 1½ to 2 hours, or when bird has browned, lower oven temperature to 350°F. Baste frequently with butter and pan drippings. If the turkey browns too much, cover it with foil.

3.   When the turkey is fully cooked, remove it from the roasting pan and keep warm. Tilt the pan so that all of the drippings run into one corner and remove as much fat as you can with a spoon.

4.   Place the pan with the defatted drippings over a stove burner on medium heat. Add Chicken Stock. Cook until all the liquid is reduced by half, scraping the bottom of the pan as you cook. Add 3 tablespoons flour, mix well, and simmer 20 minutes. (It is important that the flour be well cooked, so that the gravy does not have a floury taste.) Place in a sauceboat and pass with the carved turkey.

Makes about 12 portions

⚜⚜⚜ Stuffing

This stuffing is robust and full of flavor. Bake it separately and serve it along with the carved turkey and gravy.

3 pounds sweet Italian sausage, not in casing
1 tablespoon olive oil
4 ribs celery, cut into medium dice
2 medium Spanish onions, peeled and cut into medium dice
3 cloves garlic, peeled and mashed
3 pounds mushrooms, prepared as Duxelles (see Index)
3 medium loaves good Italian or French bread, 2 days old
4 eggs
1½–2 cups Chicken Stock (see Index)
Salt and freshly ground black pepper
1 tablespoon dried thyme

1. Preheat oven to 350°F. Spread sausage in a roasting pan and bake 30 minutes. Sausage should be brown. Pour off fat.

2. Heat olive oil in a frying pan over medium heat and sauté celery and onions 3 minutes. Add garlic and cook 1 minute. Remove to a large bowl and add Duxelles and cooked sausage.

3. Cut bread into ½-inch cubes. Place in the large bowl with other ingredients. Add eggs (you don't have to beat them separately) and Chicken Stock and mix all ingredients well with your hands, breaking up the bread as you mix. Season with salt, pepper, and thyme.

4. Place the stuffing in a greased roasting pan and bake uncovered 30 minutes at 350°F. Serve with the turkey and gravy.

Makes about 12 portions

❦❦❦ Cranberry-Orange Relish

This old favorite is simple, quick, and tasty.

    2   whole oranges
    2   pounds fresh cranberries
1½–2   cups sugar, depending on your taste

    1.   Wash, quarter, and seed oranges but do not peel. Place in food processor and chop roughly.

    2.   Wash cranberries well and add to processor. Process to a rough puree.

    3.   Remove to a glass bowl and combine with sugar. Cover and let mixture mellow in the refrigerator for 2–3 hours before serving.

Makes about 5 cups

Variation: Add one apple, seeded and quartered, to processor with oranges.

❦ Puree of Carrots with Ginger

This is a simple puree of steamed carrots, enhanced by the addition of fresh ginger.

3   bunches carrots, scrubbed and cut into ¼-inch rounds
Water to cover
2   tablespoons butter
1   teaspoon sugar
1   teaspoon grated fresh ginger
Salt and freshly ground black pepper

    1.   Place carrots in a large pot and cover with water. Add butter, sugar, and 3–4 grinds of pepper. Bring water to a boil and cook carrots until very tender, about 15 minutes. Drain.

    2.   Puree carrots in food processor until smooth. Add ginger, salt, and pepper to taste.

    3.   Boil cooking water until it is reduced to a glaze; combine glaze with the puree.

Makes 12 portions

⚜⚜⚜ Candied Sweet Potatoes

These potatoes are briefly cooked in boiling water, but the major part of their cooking takes place in the oven, where they absorb the delicious syrup that flavors them.

Potatoes
18   medium sweet potatoes
Water to cover

Syrup
½   cup corn syrup
½   cup brown sugar
¼   pound sweet butter

    1.   Preheat oven to 350°F.

    2.   Place sweet potatoes in a large pot, cover with water, and boil until half-done, or still quite firm, about 20 minutes. Drain potatoes; peel and quarter. Arrange potatoes in a shallow baking pan.

    3.   Prepare syrup: Combine all ingredients in a medium saucepan. Bring to a simmer over medium heat and continue simmering until sugar and butter are melted.

    4.   Pour syrup over potatoes. Cover pan with aluminum foil and bake 30 minutes. Uncover and bake another 15 minutes.

Makes 12 portions

❧ Steamed Green Beans

Water to cover
½ teaspoon salt
3 pounds green beans, washed and tips cut off
4 tablespoons butter
Salt and freshly ground black pepper

1. Put water and salt in a large pot and bring to boil. Add beans, cover, and cook 4–5 minutes. Remove from pot.

2. Toss with butter. Season with salt and pepper to taste.

Makes 12 portions

❧ Applesauce

20 medium apples
½ cup water
½ cup sugar
½ teaspoon ground cinnamon

1. Peel and core the apples and cut into quarters. Place in a heavy pot with water. Cook, covered, over medium heat 10 minutes, or until apples are soft. Add sugar and mix with a wooden spoon.

2. Place apple mixture in a food processor and puree until desired texture is reached. I prefer applesauce very smooth, but you can puree it briefly for a chunky texture. Add cinnamon to taste.

Makes 12 portions

A Week of Well-Planned, Moderate Dinner Menus

The menus I have listed here illustrate what this book is about: Each of these meals is delicious and exciting. None of them will make you feel that you are denying yourself the pleasure of good eating, yet they all have been planned with moderation and common sense in mind. (And they will not keep you in the kitchen all evening.)

Each menu consists of three to four courses, with the richer elements balanced by the lighter. A salad of Artichoke Hearts and Lobster is complemented by a light pasta and a dessert of fresh strawberries. A hearty Beef Stew with Winter Vegetables is preceded by Grilled Eggplant and Tomatoes with Yogurt Sauce and followed by a dessert of Grapefruit Sorbet. A menu with no rich elements, but with two moderate dishes, is the Angel Hair Pasta with Roasted Peppers, Chicken Breasts with Balsamic Vinegar, Steamed Snow Peas and Carrots, and Marinated Fruit. The fruit dessert is rated moderate because of its sugar content, but it contains no fats, cream, or egg yolks.

Whether I was dining in the fine restaurants of France or planning dinner parties at Gracie Mansion, I aimed for balance—beautiful, elegant meals that were not overly rich. You will find that balance in the menus that follow. (See Index for recipes.)

♣♣♣ Artichoke Hearts and Lobster with Raspberry Vinaigrette

♣ Angel Hair Pasta with Sun-Dried Tomatoes

♣ Fresh Strawberries

♣ Grilled Eggplant and Tomatoes with Yogurt Sauce

♣♣♣ Beef Stew with Winter Vegetables

♣ Grapefruit Sorbet

♣ Angel Hair Pasta with Roasted Peppers

♣♣ Chicken Breasts with Balsamic Vinegar

♣ Steamed Snow Peas and Carrots

♣♣ Marinated Fruit

215

♣ Mayor Koch's Favorite Pureed Mussel Soup

♣♣♣ Chicken Stuffed Under the Skin with Farmer Cheese

♣ Steamed Haricots Verts

♣ Orange Sorbet

♣ Tomatoes with Fresh Basil

♣♣ Veal Scalloppine with Calvados, Garnished with Glazed Apples

♣ Steamed Spinach

♣ Strawberries with Raspberry Puree

♣ Broiled Wild Mushrooms

♣♣ Leg of Lamb with Vegetables in One Pot

♣ Puree of Turnips and Parsnips

♣♣ Poached Pears with Two Fruit Purees

♣♣ Asparagus with Parmesan

♣ Roasted Striped Bass with Roasted Fennel

♣ Sautéed Cherry Tomatoes

♣ Fresh Melon

INDEX

Angel Hair Pasta
  with Olive Oil and Basil, 70
  with Roasted Peppers, 77
  with Sun-Dried Tomatoes, 75
  with Tomatoes, Garlic, and Basil, 71
Appetizers, 43–54
  Artichokes Steamed with Yogurt and Basil
    Sauce, 53
  Asparagus with Parmesan, 45
  Bruschetta alla Romana, 46
  Eggplant with Tomatoes, 52
  Eggplant and Tomatoes, Grilled, with
    Yogurt Sauce, 51
  Peppers, Roasted Red and Yellow, 44
  Pizza, Grilled, 54
  Tomatoes with Basil, Grilled Marinated,
    50
  Tomatoes with Fresh Basil, 46
  Vegetables, Roasted, 47
  Wild Mushrooms, Broiled, 48
Applesauce, 212
Artichoke(s)
  Hearts and Lobster with Raspberry
    Vinaigrette, 184
  Steamed with Yogurt and Basil Sauce, 53
  Veal Chops Broiled with, 140
Arugula
  with Balsamic Vinegar, 180
  and Roasted Red Pepper Salad, 180
  and Tomato Salad with Marinated
    Mussels, 181
  Veal Chops, 137
Asparagus
  with Grilled Shrimp, 111
  with Parmesan, 45

Balsamic Vinaigrette, 191
Balsamic Vinegar, Arugula with, 180
Basic Vinaigrette with Fresh Herbs, 190

Basil
  about, 25
  Fresh, Tomatoes with, 46
  Pesto, 26
  Vinaigrette, 192
  and Yogurt Sauce, 27
Bass. See Striped Bass
Batter-Fried Zucchini, 167
Beef, 147, 156–59
  Fillet of, Poached, with Horseradish Sauce
    and Roasted Vegetables, 157
  Fillet Steak au Poivre, 158
  Flank Steak, Marinated, 156
  Stew with Winter Vegetables, 159
Bibb Lettuce, Fennel with, 182
Bibb Lettuce, Goat Cheese, and Red Pepper
  Salad, 182
Blanching, about, 13
Blueberries, about, 198
Bouquet Garni, 25
Braised Fennel, 170
Braised Veal with Onions, 143
Braising, about, 13
Broiled Chicken, 124
Broiled Fish
  Lemon Butter for, 6
  Lemon-Oil Topping for, 6
Broiled Flounder, Whole Baby, 87
Broiled Lobster with Lemon Butter, 113
Broiled Shad, 86
Broiled Veal Chops with Artichokes, 140
Broiled Wild Mushrooms, 48
Broiling, about, 5–6
Brown Veal Stock, 34
Bruschetta alla Romana, 46
Butternut Squash and Parsnip Puree, 164

Caesar Salad, 186
Candied Sweet Potatoes, 211

217

Cantaloupe and Honeydew, about, 199
Carrot(s)
  Grilled, 165
  Puree, 164
  Puree of, with Ginger, 210
  and Snow Peas, Steamed, 166
  and Zucchini, Steamed, 166
Chanterelles, Fettuccine with, 72
Cherries (Bing, White), about, 198
Chervil, about, 27
Chervil Vinaigrette, 190
Chicken, 121–30
  Broiled, 124
  Cutlets with Rosemary, 128
  Roasted with Black Peppercorns, 122
  Roasted with Thirty-Five Cloves of
    Garlic, 123
  Sautéed with Fresh Herbs, 125
  Scallops Sautéed with Mint, 130
  Stock, 35
  Stuffed Under the Skin with Farmer
    Cheese, 126
Chicken Breasts
  with Balsamic Vinegar, 128
  Sautéed with Pesto, 130
  Stuffed with Duxelles, 127
  with Wild Mushrooms and Persillade, 129
Chives, about, 27
Citrus Drink, Gogol-Mogol, 204
Clam(s)
  Chowder, Manhattan, 60
  Steamed Littleneck, with Garlic and
    Parsley, 108
  Steamed Littleneck, with Pesto, 108
Court Bouillon, 37
Cranberry-Orange Relish, 210
Cucumber, Tomato, and Onion Salad, 185
Curry, Lamb, with Apples, 151

Desserts, 197–204. See also name of fresh
    fruit
  Applesauce, 212
  Grapefruit Sorbet, 199
  Marinated Fruit, 201
  Peaches, Elaine London's Home-Canned,
    203
  Pears, Poached, with Two Fruit Purees,
    200
  Strawberries with Raspberry Puree, 202
Dill, about, 28
Dinner-in-Itself Fish Soup, 62
Dinner Menus, 215-16
Dressing. See Salad Dressing
Duxelles, 22
Duxelles, Chicken Breasts Stuffed with, 127

Eggplant
  Roasted, 168
  Puree, 169
  with Tomatoes, 52
  and Tomatoes, Grilled with Yogurt Sauce,
    51
Elaine London's Home-Canned Peaches, 203
Endive and Watercress Salad, 183
Extra-Light Dressing, 192

Fennel
  about, 28
  with Bibb Lettuce, 182
  Braised, 170
  Roasted, Roasted Striped Bass with, 100
Fettuccine
  with Chanterelles, 72
  with Goat Cheese, Basil, and Red
    Peppers, 74
  with Porcini, 80
  Primavera with Ricotta Cheese, 76
  with Tomato Sauce and Steamed
    Vegetables, 73
Fillet of Beef, Poached, with Horseradish
    Sauce and Roasted Vegetables, 157
Fillet Steak au Poivre, 158
Fish, 85–103. See also Shellfish
  Flounder, Whole Baby, Broiled, 87
  Halibut, Poached on a Bed of Grilled
    Leeks, 88
  Marinade for, 7
  Red Snapper with Saffron, 89
  Salmon
    Chunks, Grilled, 52
    Grilled Marinated Scallops of, 96
    en Papillote, 94
    Poached with Dill and Yogurt Sauce, 91
    Poached with Sorrel Sauce, 92
    Roasted, 90
    Sautéed Scallops of, 95
    Steaks with Black Beans, 93
  Sardines, Grilled, 95
  Shad, Broiled, 86
  Sole, Grilled, 97
  Sole, Steamed Fillet of, with Duxelles,
    Wrapped in Spinach, 98
  Soup, Dinner-in-Itself, 62
  Stock or Fumet, 36
  Striped Bass, Roasted, 99
  Striped Bass, Roasted with Roasted
    Fennel, 100
  Swordfish en Brochette, 101
  Toppings for, 6
  Trout with Lemon and Butter, 102
  Tuna, Grilled Marinated, 103
Flank Steak, Marinated, 156
Flounder, Whole Baby, Broiled, 87
Fruit. See name of fruit
Fruit, Marinated, 201
Fumet or Fish Stock, 36
Fusilli with Zucchini, Prosciutto, and
    Romano, 81

Garlic
  about, 23
  Roasted, 24
  and Shiitake Mushrooms, Tomatoes
    Stuffed with, 173
  and Yogurt Dressing, 193
Gazpacho, 65
Goat Cheese, Bibb Lettuce, and Red Pepper
    Salad, 182
Gogol-Mogol, 204
Grapefruit Sorbet, 199
Green Beans. See Haricots Verts

Green Beans, Steamed, 212
Green Peppercorns, Medallions of Lamb
    with, 149
Grilled Butterflied Leg of Lamb, 154
Grilled Carrots, 165
Grilled Eggplant and Tomatoes with Yogurt
    Sauce, 51
Grilled Marinated Scallops of Salmon, 96
Grilled Marinated Tomatoes with Basil, 50
Grilled Marinated Tuna, 103
Grilled Pizza, 54
Grilled Salmon Chunks, 52
Grilled Sardines, 95
Grilled Scallops, 117
Grilled Shrimp with Asparagus, 111
Grilled Sole, 97
Grilling, about, 8

Halibut Poached on a Bed of Grilled Leeks,
    88
Haricots Verts Salad, 185
Haricots Verts, Steamed, 171
Herbs
    about, 25–30
    Basil, 25
    Bouquet Garni, 25
    Chervil, 27
    Chives, 27
    Dill, 28
    Fennel, 28
    Mint, 28
    Oregano, 29
    Parsley, 29
    Peppercorns, 30
    Persillade, 29
    Rosemary, 30
    Sorrel, 30
    Tarragon, 30
    Thyme, 30
Honeydew and Cantaloupe, about, 199
Horseradish, about, 24
Horseradish Sauce, 24

Kitchen Essentials, about, 14–15

Lamb, 147–55
    Curry with Apples, 151
    Leg of, Grilled Butterflied, 154
    Leg of, Roast, 153
    Leg of, with Vegetables in One Pot, 152
    Medallions of, with Green Peppercorns,
        149
    Medallions of, with Wild Mushrooms, 150
    Patties, Leftover, with Yogurt and Parsley
        Sauce, 155
    Rack of, 148
Leeks, Grilled, Poached Halibut on a Bed
    of, 88
Leeks and Mushrooms, Roasted Veal Chops
    on, 138
Leftover Lamb Patties with Yogurt and
    Parsley Sauce, 155
Leg of Lamb with Vegetables in One Pot,
    152
Lemonade, Mint, 28

Lettuce. *See* Bibb Lettuce
Light Pesto Sauce, 27
Light Tomato Sauce, 20
Lobster and Artichoke Hearts with
    Raspberry Vinaigrette, 184
Lobster, Broiled with Lemon Butter, 113

Manhattan Clam Chowder, 60
Marinade
    for Fish and Shrimp, 7
    Veal Chop, 9
Marinated Flank Steak, 156
Marinated Fruit, 201
Marinated Grilled Scallops of Salmon, 96
Marinated Grilled Tomatoes with Basil, 50
Marinated Grilled Tuna, 103
Marinated Mussels, Arugula and Tomato
    Salad with, 181
Marinated Zucchini, 49
Marinating, about, 14
Mayor Koch's Favorite Pureed Mussel Soup,
    58
Mayor's Cold Remedy, Gogol-Mogol, 204
Mayor's Thanksgiving Dinner, 207-12
Medallions of Lamb with Green
    Peppercorns, 149
Medallions of Lamb with Wild Mushrooms,
    150
Melange of Steamed Vegetables, 174
Minestrone, 63
Mint, about, 28
Mint Lemonade, 28
Morels, Veal Medallions with, 134
Mushroom(s). *See also* Wild Mushrooms
    about, 21
    Duxelles, 22
    Soup, 61
Mussel(s)
    Marinated, Arugula and Tomato Salad
        with, 181
    Provencale, 109
    Soup, Pureed, Mayor Koch's Favorite, 58
    Soup with Saffron, 59
    in White Wine, 110

Onion, Cucumber, and Tomato Salad, 185
Onions, about, 23
Orange(s)
    Cranberry Relish, 210
    Temple, about, 199
    Vinaigrette, 191
Oregano, about, 29
Osso Buco, 141
Oysters and Scallops in Papillote with
    Thyme, 114

Papardelle with Leeks and Sun-Dried
    Tomatoes, 79
Parsley
    about, 29
    Steamed Potatoes, 171
    and Yogurt Sauce, 29
Parsnip Puree and Butternut Squash, 164
Parsnips and Turnips, Puree of, 176

Pasta, 69–81
  Angel Hair
    with Olive Oil and Basil, 70
    with Roasted Peppers, 77
    with Sun-Dried Tomatoes, 75
    with Tomatoes, Garlic, and Basil, 71
  Fettuccine
    with Chanterelles, 72
    with Goat Cheese, Basil, and Red
      Peppers, 74
    with Porcini, 80
    Primavera with Ricotta Cheese, 76
    with Tomato Sauce and Steamed
      Vegetables, 73
  Fusilli with Zucchini, Prosciutto, and
    Romano, 81
  Papardelle with Leeks and Sun-Dried
    Tomatoes, 79
  with Pesto, 26
  with Shiitake Mushrooms, 78
Peaches, about, 197
Peaches, Elaine London's Home-Canned,
  203
Pears, about, 198
Pears, Poached, with Two Fruit Purees, 200
Pepper(s)
  about, 22
  Red, Fettuccine with Goat Cheese, Basil,
    and, 74
  Red, Goat Cheese, and Bibb Lettuce
    Salad, 182
  Red and Yellow, Scallops Sautéed with,
    118
  Red and Yellow, Veal Chops with, 139
  Roasted, 22
  Roasted, Angel Hair Pasta with, 77
  Roasted Red, and Arugula Salad, 180
  Roasted, Steamed Scallops in Spinach
    Leaves on, 115
Peppercorns, about, 30
Persillade, 29
Pesto, 26
  Chicken Sautéed with, 130
  Pasta with, 26
  Sauce, Light, 27
Pizza, Grilled, 54
Poached Fillet of Beef with Horseradish
  Sauce and Roasted Vegetables, 157
Poached Halibut on a Bed of Grilled Leeks,
  88
Poached Pears with Two Fruit Purees, 200
Poached Salmon with Dill and Yogurt
  Sauce, 91
Poached Salmon with Sorrel Sauce, 92
Poaching, about, 11–12
Porcini, Fettuccine with, 80
Potatoes, Parsley Steamed, 171
Potatoes, Sweet, Candied, 211
Pot Roast of Veal with Pearl Onions, 142
Puree of Carrots with Ginger, 210
Puree, Eggplant, 169
Puree, Raspberry, Strawberries with, 202
Puree of Turnips and Parsnips, 176
Pureed Mussel Soup, Mayor Koch's Favorite,
  58
Pureed Vegetable Soup, 64

Rack of Lamb, 148
Raspberry(ies)
  about, 198
  Puree, Strawberries with, 202
  Vinaigrette, Artichoke Hearts and Lobster
    with, 184
Ratatouille, 175
Recipes, about fat content of, 39
Red Peppers. See Peppers
Red Snapper with Saffron, 89
Relish, Cranberry-Orange, 210
Roast Leg of Lamb, 153
Roast Turkey with Gravy, 208
Roasted Chicken with Black Peppercorns,
  122
Roasted Chicken with Thirty-Five Cloves of
  Garlic, 123
Roasted Eggplant, 168
Roasted Garlic, 24
Roasted Peppers, 22
Roasted Peppers, Angel Hair Pasta with, 77
Roasted Red Pepper and Arugula Salad, 180
Roasted Red and Yellow Peppers, 44
Roasted Salmon, 90
Roasted Shiitake Mushrooms, 21
Roasted Striped Bass, 99
Roasted Striped Bass with Roasted Fennel,
  100
Roasted Veal Chops on a Bed of Leeks and
  Mushrooms, 138
Roasted Vegetables, 47
Roasting, about, 10
Rosemary, about, 30

Salad, 179–86
  Artichoke Hearts and Lobster with
    Raspberry Vinaigrette, 184
  Arugula with Balsamic Vinegar, 180
  Arugula and Roasted Red Pepper, 180
  Bibb Lettuce, Goat Cheese, and Red
    Pepper, 182
  Caesar, 186
  Cucumber, Tomato, and Onion, 185
  Endive and Watercress, 183
  Fennel with Bibb Lettuce, 182
  Haricots Verts, 185
  Tomato, 183
  Tomato and Arugula with Marinated
    Mussels, 181
Salad Dressing, 189–93. See also Vinaigrette
  Extra Light, 192
  Yogurt and Garlic, 193
Salmon
  Chunks, Grilled, 52
  Grilled Marinated Scallops of, 96
  Marinade for, 7
  en Papillote, 94
  Poached with Dill and Yogurt Sauce, 91
  Poached with Sorrel Sauce, 92
  Roasted, 90
  Sautéed Scallops of, 95
  Steaks with Black Beans, 93
Sardines, Grilled, 95

Sauce
    Horseradish, 24
    Pesto, 26
    Pesto, Light, 27
    Tomato, Light, 20
    Yogurt and Basil, 27
    Yogurt and Parsley, 29
Sautéed Cherry Tomatoes, 172
Sautéed Chicken with Fresh Herbs, 125
Sautéed Chicken with Pesto, 130
Sautéed Chicken Scallops with Mint, 130
Sautéed Scallops with Red and Yellow
    Peppers, 118
Sautéed Scallops of Salmon, 95
Sautéing, about, 12-13
Scallop(s)
    Brochettes, 116
    Grilled, 117
    and Oysters in Papillote with Thyme, 114
    Sautéed, with Red and Yellow Peppers,
        118
    Steamed, in Spinach Leaves, on a Bed of
        Roasted Peppers, 115
Shad, Broiled, 86
Shellfish, 107-118. See also Fish
    Clam Chowder, Manhattan, 60
    Clams, Steamed Littleneck, with Garlic
        and Parsley, 108
    Clams, Steamed Littleneck, with Pesto,
        108
    Lobster and Artichoke Hearts with
        Raspberry Vinaigrette, 184
    Lobster, Broiled with Lemon Butter, 113
    Mussel(s)
        Marinated, Arugula and Tomato Salad
            with, 181
        Provencale, 109
        Soup, Pureed, Mayor Koch's Favorite, 58
        Soup with Saffron, 59
        in White Wine, 110
    Scallop(s)
        Brochettes, 116
        Grilled, 117
        and Oysters in Papillote with Thyme,
            114
        Sautéed, with Red and Yellow Peppers,
            118
        Steamed, in Spinach Leaves, on a Bed
            of Roasted Peppers, 115
    Shrimp
        with Coriander, 112
        Grilled, Asparagus with, 111
        Marinade for, 7
        Steamed, with Ginger, 112
Shiitake Mushrooms
    and Leeks, Roasted Veal Chops on, 138
    Pasta with, 78
    Roasted, 21
    and Roasted Garlic, Tomatoes Stuffed
        with, 173
Snow Peas and Carrots, Steamed, 166
Sole, Grilled, 97
Sole, Steamed Fillet of, with Duxelles,
    Wrapped in Spinach, 98

Sorbet, Grapefruit, 199
Sorrel, about, 30
Soup, 57-65
    Fish, Dinner-in-Itself, 62
    Gazpacho, 65
    Manhattan Clam Chowder, 60
    Minestrone, 63
    Mushroom, 61
    Mussel, Pureed, Mayor Koch's Favorite, 58
    Mussel, with Saffron, 59
    Vegetable, Pureed, 64
Spinach, Steamed, 172
Steak. See Beef
Steamed Artichokes with Yogurt and Basil
    Sauce, 53
Steamed Fillet of Sole with Duxelles,
    Wrapped in Spinach, 98
Steamed Green Beans, 212
Steamed Haricots Verts, 171
Steamed Littleneck Clams with Garlic and
    Parsley, 108
Steamed Littleneck Clams with Pesto, 108
Steamed Parsley Potatoes, 171
Steamed Scallops in Spinach Leaves, on a
    Bed of Roasted Peppers, 115
Steamed Shrimp with Ginger, 112
Steamed Snow Peas and Carrots, 166
Steamed Spinach, 172
Steamed Vegetables, Fettuccine with Tomato
    Sauce and, 73
Steamed Vegetables, Melange of, 174
Steamed Zucchini and Carrots, 166
Steaming, about, 11
Stocks, 33-37
    Chicken, 35
    Court Bouillon, 37
    Fish or Fumet, 36
    Veal, Brown, 34
Strawberries, about, 198
Strawberries with Raspberry Puree, 202
Striped Bass, Roasted, 99
Striped Bass, Roasted, with Roasted Fennel,
    100
Stuffing (Turkey), 209
Sweet Potatoes, Candied, 211
Swordfish en Brochette, 101
Swordfish, Marinade for, 7

Tarragon, about, 30
Temple Oranges, about, 199
Thanksgiving Dinner, 207-12
Thyme, about, 30
Tomato(es)
    about, 20
    and Arugula Salad with Marinated
        Mussels, 181
    with Basil, Fresh, 46
    with Basil, Grilled Marinated, 50
    Bruschetta alla Romana, 46
    Cherry, Sautéed, 172
    Cucumber, and Onion Salad, 185
    with Eggplant, 52
    and Eggplant, Grilled with Yogurt Sauce,
        51

Salad, 183
Sauce, Light, 20
Stuffed with Roasted Garlic and Shiitake
    Mushrooms, 173
Sun-Dried, Angel Hair Pasta with, 75
Sun-Dried, Papardelle with Leeks and, 79
Trout with Lemon and Butter, 102
Tuna, Grilled Marinated, 103
Tuna, Marinade for, 7
Turkey, Roast, with Gravy, 208
Turkey Stuffing, 209
Turnips and Parsnips, Puree of, 176

Veal, 133–143
    Braised, with Onions, 143
    Chop(s)
        Arugula, 137
        Broiled, with Artichokes, 140
        Marinade, 9
        with Red and Yellow Peppers, 139
        Roasted, on a Bed of Leeks and
            Mushrooms, 138
    Medallions with Morels, 134
    Osso Buco, 141
    Pot Roast with Pearl Onions, 142
    Scalloppine with Calvados, Garnished
        with Glazed Apples, 136
    Scalloppine with Coriander, 135
    Stock, Brown, 34
Vegetable(s), 163–76. *See also* name of
    vegetable
    in One Pot, Leg of Lamb with, 152
    Ratatouille, 175
    Roasted, 47
    Soup, Pureed, 64
    Steamed, Fettuccine with Tomato Sauce
        and, 73

Steamed, Melange of, 174
Winter, Beef Stew with, 159
Vinaigrette
    Balsamic, 191
    Basic, with Fresh Herbs, 190
    Basil, 192
    Chervil, 190
    Orange, 191
    Raspberry, Artichoke Hearts and Lobster
        with, 184

Watercress and Endive Salad, 183
Wild Mushrooms. *See also* Mushrooms
    Broiled, 48
    Chanterelles, Fettuccine with, 72
    Lamb Medallions with, 150
    Morels, Veal Medallions with, 134
    and Persillade, Chicken Breasts with, 129
    Porcini, Fettuccine with, 80
    Shiitake
        and Leeks, Roasted Veal Chops on, 138
        Pasta with, 78
        Roasted, 21
        and Roasted Garlic, Tomatoes Stuffed
            with, 173

Yellow Peppers. *See* Peppers
Yogurt
    and Basil Sauce, 27
    and Garlic Dressing, 193
    and Parsley Sauce, 29

Zucchini
    Batter-Fried, 167
    and Carrots, Steamed, 166
    Marinated, 49
    Prosciutto, and Romano, Fusilli with, 81